Folk Tales for Fearless Girls

Retold by
Samantha Newman

Illustrated by
Khoa Le

ARCTURUS

This edition published in 2025 by Arcturus Publishing Limited
26/27 Bickels Yard, 151–153 Bermondsey Street,
London SE1 3HA

Copyright © Arcturus Holdings Limited

All rights reserved. No part of this publication may be reproduced, stored in a retrieval system, or transmitted, in any form or by any means, electronic, mechanical, photocopying, recording, or otherwise, without prior written permission in accordance with the provisions of the Copyright Act 1956 (as amended). Any person or persons who do any unauthorized act in relation to this publication may be liable to criminal prosecution and civil claims for damages.

Author: Samantha Newman
Illustrator: Khoa Le
Editors: Becca Clunes and Donna Gregory
Designer: Allie Oldfield
Design Manager: Jessica Holliland
Managing Editor: Joe Harris

ISBN: 978-1-3988-2005-0
CH010693NT
Supplier 29, Date 1224, PI 00009309
Printed in China

Contents

Introduction 5

Ayanna and the Magic Cooking Pot 9
  Based on a Swahili story, from eastern Africa

Catherine and Her Destiny 16
  Based on an Italian tale

Elisa and the Swans 25
  Based on a traditional German story

How the Moon Was Made 32
  Based on Maori myths

Iara and Her Brothers 40
  Based on a tale from the Tupi people of Brazil

The Green Serpent 49
  Based on a French tale

The King and His Daughters 56
  Based on a story from northern India

The Little Sister of the Giants 65
  Based on Brazilian myths

Timun Mas 72
  Based on a traditional Javanese tale

Leelinau, the Lost Daughter 81
  Based on a story from the Chippewa people of the Great Lakes, North America

Anush, the Golden Maiden 88
  Based on a traditional Armenian folk tale

Princess Pyeonggang 97
  Based on a story from South Korea

Savitri's Love 104
  Based on a traditional folk tale from western India

Tuya, the Clever Daughter-in-Law 113
  Based on a story from Mongolia

Nayece, the Mother of All 120
  Based on a traditional Turkana folk tale from north-eastern Africa

Introduction

Folk tales aren't like most stories written in books. They are much, much older than the other stories you will have read or heard. They have been told out loud, from one person to another, for hundreds or even thousands of years. Some can even be traced back to a time before humans figured out systems of writing and reading.

Folk tales aren't set in stone, though. They are always changing—because each storyteller will add something of their own to a tale, whether they mean to or not. You might say that they are gifts—passed from one friend to another, or from parent to child.

Every world culture has its own traditional tales featuring characters they know and love. When those folk tales are written down, they can be shared with other communities. Sharing like this helps people from different places to understand each other—and to see how much they have in common.

All of the stories in this collection were created for different reasons, and they each contain important messages. Some of them were made up to explain why the natural world works the way it does, such as the story of *How the Moon Was Made* from Aotearoa (also known as New Zealand). Some were told to explain how a particular group of people came to live in a certain place, like the Turkana people in *Nayece, the Mother of All*.

But the most important messages of all are about what is right and what is wrong. Many of these stories feature villains who are selfish, jealous, and cruel. In these tales, we see these villains get their comeuppance, reminding us not to behave the same way as they do.

And to show us a good way to live, we look to the heroines of our tales. Although they are from all around the world and their stories are very different, they all have something in common—they are all brave and strong.

When we think of someone brave and strong, we often think of someone who is physically strong, standing tall to face a fearsome enemy. But the truth is that that is only one type of strength and one type of bravery.

For example, it takes bravery to do not what everyone else wants you to do, but to follow your heart and find your own path in life. We see this quiet strength in Leelinau's tale from North America.

It also takes bravery to remain kind and generous even when those around you

are trying to hurt you. We see this gentle strength in many of our stories, including Ayanna's tale from Kenya, Lakia's story from India, and in the story of Anush from Armenia.

Then, of course, there is the bravery and strength to be found in protecting others, whether that is your family, such as in Elisa's and Savitri's tales, or perhaps an entire kingdom, as we see in Princess Pyeonggang's story.

On top of all these fine examples, we also have the more traditional representation of the bravery and strength of the warriors and pioneers, such as in Iana's tale of revenge from Brazil.

We would like to draw our readers' attention to one final point. In many traditional stories—including several of the tales in this collection—stepmothers are cast in the role of villain. We have left this unchanged for the purposes of this collection but would like to remind our readers that in the real world, most stepmothers are patient, kind, and every bit as fearless as any fictional heroines.

We hope that you enjoy reading these richly diverse tales that celebrate girls from all different walks of life, from all around the world. We hope they make you gasp, make you smile, and maybe even make you feel a little bit fearless yourself!

Happy reading!

Ayanna and the Magic Cooking Pot

Based on a Swahili story, from eastern Africa

A long time ago, in the land that we now know as Kenya, there lived a young girl named Ayanna and her brother, Kito. Their father, Mwanga, had been unwell for many years, and one day, it was time to say goodbye to him, for he was dying.

Mwanga smiled at Ayanna and Kito. "My dear children, I do not have much to leave you. Only this house and everything in it—or my fond blessing. Which would you rather have?"

"The house and everything in it, of course," said Kito, greedily. "I want that."

Mwanga glanced at Ayanna. "Do you also want the house, Ayanna?"

Ayanna took Mwanga's hand, with tears in her eyes. "No, Father. Nothing in the world could be more important to me than having your blessing."

Mwanga smiled once more. "Then you shall have it, my dear. And Kito, when your mother dies, the house will be yours."

As their father died, both of the siblings felt that they had been given the best gift.

Not long after their father had passed away, their mother became ill. As she lay dying, she called the children to her and asked the same question. "My darling children: Would you rather have the house or my blessing?"

"Your blessing, dear mother!" Ayanna cried. "For I shall miss you so!"

"It is yours," her mother said, caressing her face.

"I would like the house, Mother," Kito added. "And everything in it, like Father said."

"Then it is yours, but I hope you will also take care of your sister," said his mother. She took her final breath and died.

Kito took over the house. "It was left to me, so you can't live here," he told Ayanna, unkindly. "You must stay in the smaller hut with the hole in the roof. I will give you a cooking pot and a pitcher for water, and that's it."

Ayanna took her pot and her pitcher and sat in the doorway of her leaky hut. She knew that her parents would be watching over her, and she was sure that she would be okay, somehow. But as the shadows began to lengthen, Ayanna began to feel worried. She had nothing to eat.

"Ayanna! Please may I borrow your cooking pot?" came an urgent-sounding voice. It was Jioni, one of Ayanna's late mother's friends. Jioni was looking stressed. "My pot cracked just as I was about to make dinner for the family."

"Of course," Ayanna said, for she would always take care of others.

Jioni was so grateful that once she had made her dinner, she gifted Ayanna with some corn to say thank you.

Ayanna took her pot back to the tumbledown hut and cooked the corn for her own dinner.

The next night, someone else's pot had broken and once again, they asked to borrow Ayanna's pot in exchange for some food. This

happened night after night. The more Ayanna helped others, the more help she received.

One day, she found a pumpkin seed in the dirt. She dug the earth outside her hut and planted the seed. The seed sprouted, and soon Ayanna had an entire flourishing pumpkin patch. She was able to start selling pumpkins to the other villagers, and everyone said they were some of the tastiest pumpkins they had ever eaten.

Kito saw Ayanna doing so well after she had started with just a leaky hut, a cooking pot, and a pitcher. He himself had married a rich woman and was living a good life, but he still felt jealous of what his sister had built for herself. One night, he sneaked out and stole her cooking pot and water pitcher.

When Ayanna woke up, she was dismayed to find that her pot and pitcher were missing, but she was earning enough from her pumpkin patch to buy new ones.

When Kito spotted her carrying the new pot and pitcher home, he felt even angrier.

Meanwhile, Kito's wife, Nalah, had heard about the delicious pumpkins and wanted to try them for herself. She took a handful of grain and went to Ayanna. "I wish to buy a pumpkin from you," she said.

Ayanna's eyes widened. She knew who Nalah was, even though Kito hadn't introduced them. "Why, you are my brother's wife!" she exclaimed. "Keep your grain. I will give you a pumpkin for free, of course."

Nalah thanked her, took the pumpkin home, and ate it. It was indeed the most delicious pumpkin she had ever tasted, and she went to bed that night still thinking about it. The next morning, she went back to Ayanna. "Dear sister, can I have another pumpkin?" she asked.

"I'm sorry, Nalah," Ayanna replied. "I sold the last of my ripe pumpkins yesterday after you left. The next batch won't be ready for a few days."

Nalah was quite a spoiled lady and was used to getting what she wanted. "I'll give you grain," she pouted.

"That's very kind, but I can't make the pumpkins ripen any faster," Ayanna said. "Come back in a few days, and you shall have a beautiful big one."

Nalah stomped home. "Your horrible sister won't sell me any of her pumpkins, even though she had lots, and she is giving them to all the other ladies for free," she lied to Kito.

Kito was filled with rage. "How dare she treat my wife so poorly?" he yelled as he marched over to Ayanna's with a knife. "Since you wouldn't give my wife a pumpkin, I am going to cut down all your plants!" he shouted.

"That's not true!" Ayanna protested. But Kito wouldn't listen. He hacked at all the pumpkin vines.

Ayanna put her hand on one of the last vines. "No, if you want to kill my plants, you will have to cut my hand off, too!" she cried.

"Your choice," Kito shrugged. He raised his knife—and cut Ayanna's hand clean off!

Ayanna fled into the forest, distraught and in pain.

She wandered the forest for many moons, eating berries and nuts, and drinking from cool streams, until she met a prince from the next town.

"Tell me, Ayanna, why do you look so sad?" the prince asked, after they had introduced themselves.

When Ayanna told him her story, the prince was moved with pity—and admiration for Ayanna's beautiful spirit. They became good friends and ended up getting married. Ayanna went to live with the prince and his parents in their palace in the town beyond the forest. They had a baby together, and for a while, Ayanna was very happy.

Meanwhile, Kito had lost all that their parents had given him. He turned up in Ayanna's new town one day and was furious when he heard that his sister had married the prince. He marched straight to see the king and queen. "I am from Ayanna's town. Do you know why she only has one hand?" he asked.

"She told us her wicked brother cut it off," said the queen.

Kito laughed. "She is a liar. Her hand was cut off because she is a witch."

Now, the prince was away on a long journey at this time, so the king and queen could not talk to him. But they were alarmed by Kito's words and decided that they needed to get this dangerous witch away from their family. They cast her out into the woods with her baby, with nothing but a single cooking pot.

Ayanna was devastated to be left with nothing once again. She hoped that her parents still watched over her, but she found it hard to believe.

She wandered the forest, foraging for food. And that evening, when she sat down and was about to cook, a spotted black snake came slithering out of the trees. Ayanna was alarmed and clutched her baby close.

"Please help me," said the snake. "A bigger snake is looking for me. Can I hide in your cooking pot?"

Ayanna was surprised to meet a talking snake, but she said, "Yes, you may."

The snake crawled in. Ayanna hid behind a bush and held her breath. A moment later, a huge green snake slithered by and disappeared into the trees beyond.

"Thank you," said the little black snake. "In return, let me tell you that if you bathe in the pond over there, good things will happen."

Ayanna was surprised but reasoned that life couldn't get much worse. So, she did as the snake said. When she climbed out of the pond, to her shock, her severed hand had grown back!

"Oh, thank you!" she said to the snake.

"Come with me to meet my parents," said the snake. "I know they will want to give you gifts of their own for saving me."

Ayanna followed the little black snake to a great nest, deep in the forest. There, his parents greeted her warmly.

"As thanks for saving our son, I gift you with this magic ring," said his father. "It will provide you with food, shelter, and clothing for you and your baby."

"And I give you this casket," said his mother. "It will ensure that you are safe, always."

Ayanna was touched by their generosity. She took her gifts and went to the edge of the forest, overlooking the town where her prince lived. There, she used her magic ring to create a lovely little house, comfortable clothes, and as much food as she and her baby could eat.

When her husband returned home, his parents introduced him to Kito, their new advisor, and told him what they had done. The prince was furious. He stormed to the forest to look for Ayanna and eventually found her in her house. Together, they returned to the palace and revealed Kito's lies. He was thrown out of town and left with nothing.

Ayanna lived happily ever after. She always helped others when she could, and that help always came back to her in time.

Catherine and Her Destiny

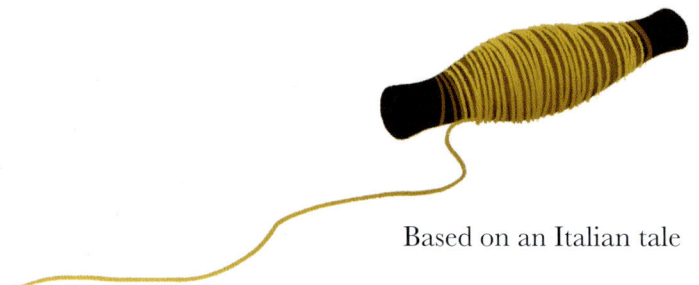

Based on an Italian tale

Once upon a time, in Italy, there lived a young girl named Catherine. She was the daughter of a rich merchant. Catherine loved to sew, and she would always make the most beautiful garments using fabric and threads that her father had brought back from all over the world.

One day, when Catherine was sewing alone in her room, the door suddenly opened. Standing on the threshold was a very tall, beautiful woman. She was wearing a long, flowing silver dress that shimmered like a rainbow when she moved. In her hands, she held a little golden wheel. The woman walked toward Catherine, smiling as if they were old friends.

"Catherine! I have a question I would like to ask you. I hope you don't mind?"

Catherine was a polite girl, and even though she was shocked by the lady's sudden appearance, she shook her head. "No, I don't mind."

The lady smiled again. "Excellent. The question is: Would you rather have a happy youth or a happy old age?"

Catherine frowned. "What an odd question!" she exclaimed. But she got into the spirit of the game. "I suppose if I chose the youth then I have only bad things to come. So, I would choose happy old age, so I have something to look forward to."

"Very well!" the lady said. She turned the little golden wheel in her hands and left the room as quickly as she had arrived.

Catherine shrugged and went back to her sewing. She didn't think of the woman again.

The day after this strange meeting, when Catherine and her father were having breakfast, a messenger came dashing into the room with a face as pale as milk.

"Sir, your ships," he panted. "They have all sunk in a storm."

It was Catherine's father's turn to go pale. "Everything I had was on those ships. We are ruined!"

Catherine jumped up and put an arm around him. "Oh, Father, I'm sure there is something to be done," she said.

But her father shook his head. The shock of losing all his worldly goods was too much for his heart to bear. He clutched at his chest, and a moment later, he tumbled to the floor, dead.

Poor Catherine was left alone in the world, without a penny to her name. She knew she would have to find some way to earn her living. She packed up her clothes, her little sewing kit, and some food and set off into the streets of the town.

As luck would have it, one of the noble ladies of the town spotted poor Catherine and decided to take pity on her and she employed her as a maid. Catherine was so grateful. The lady was a kind mistress, and she was particularly impressed by Catherine's sewing skills. Even a simple darn looked like beautiful embroidery in Catherine's hands.

One day, the lady had to travel out of town. "Catherine, I am going to have to lock up the house with you inside," the lady said. "I've heard there are thieves in the area, and I don't want them to steal anything while I am away."

A little while after the lady left, Catherine sat by a sunny window, sewing, when the door burst open. To Catherine's shock, it was the tall lady in the shimmery gown again.

"Finally, I have found you!" the lady exclaimed.

"Who are you?" Catherine demanded. "And how did you get in? My mistress locked the doors!"

The lady grinned. "There is no lock in the world that can keep me out. I am your Destiny, Catherine. Remember? You asked for a happy old age. Therefore, you must suffer in your youth."

"That is why my father died?" Catherine gasped.

Her Destiny nodded. "Yes, and that is why I am here to end this rather comfortable position you have found for yourself."

Cackling with glee, Catherine's Destiny went to where the lady of the house kept all her finest clothes and ripped them into tiny pieces.

Catherine cried out with horror. "My mistress will think I did that!"

"Exactly," chuckled Catherine's Destiny.

Catherine was so scared about getting in trouble that she fled the house. She ran to the next town and found a new house to work in. Once again, her employer was pleased with her sewing skills. But to her distress, Destiny found her much more quickly the second time and did the same thing. Once again, Catherine fled in fear of being punished.

For seven years, Catherine moved from house to house, working until her Destiny caught up with her each time. During the seventh year, Catherine began working at the house of Lady Leone. It just so happened that Lady Leone had come to an arrangement with her own Destiny some years earlier, that she would provide her with daily bread in exchange for being left alone. One of Catherine's duties was to carry the bread up a mountain each day and leave it for Lady Leone's Destiny.

Catherine only wished she could make such a deal with her own Destiny. One day, when she climbed the mountain, instead of leaving the bread, she waited for Lady Leone's Destiny.

The Destiny arrived. She was a regal figure, with glowing auburn hair. "Why do you wait, young Catherine?" she asked when she saw Catherine standing there.

"I wish to ask you to speak to my Destiny," Catherine begged. "Please could you make her leave me alone. She has ruined my life, and I live in fear for the next time she finds me."

Lady Leone's Destiny frowned as Catherine told her the whole story. "A Destiny is not supposed to behave so cruelly," she said. "I will speak to your Destiny, Catherine, and see that she makes it up to you. Meet me here tomorrow."

The next day, Catherine returned to the top of the mountain. Lady Leone's Destiny was already waiting there, with her hand clamped around the arm of Catherine's own, very sulky-looking Destiny.

As Catherine approached, her Destiny stuck out a hand. "Here, this is for you. It will help you in your time of need."

Catherine took what she held out. It was a bobbin of golden silk.

"Very good, now you can go," Lady Leone's Destiny said. Catherine's Destiny marched away, still looking resentful.

Catherine took the bobbin of silk back down the mountain, unsure as to how it was supposed to make up for what her Destiny had done.

A few weeks later, the king of the realm was getting married. He was very fond of fine clothes, and for his wedding, he had ordered his most expensive and elaborate outfit yet. However, the tailors ran out of golden silk to finish it off. They put out a call to the whole kingdom. Anyone who had golden silk could bring it to the palace for a handsome reward.

Catherine took her golden silk and walked to the palace. When she arrived, the king and his tailors were waiting in the throne room, surrounded by piles of discarded thread. The king was holding his head in his hands. "It's hopeless. We'll never find the right shade!"

Catherine approached, holding out her bobbin of silk. "Please, your majesty, might this work?"

The king's eyes widened as he saw the silk. "That looks perfect!"

One of the tailors held it up against the outfit. "It is, Sir!" he cried. "A perfect match."

"I will give you its weight in gold," the king said to Catherine. He had weighing scales brought forth and put the silk on one side. However, no matter how much gold he piled up on the other side, the silk always seemed to be heavier.

"Your Majesty, we have run out of gold!" one of the tailors said, nervously.

"But I must have this silk," the king said. He reached up to his head and put his crown in the scales. Finally, they balanced.

"But you cannot give your crown away!" gasped the tailors.

The king squinted at Catherine. "I hope this isn't a trick. Where did you get this silk from, anyway?"

"It isn't a trick, I promise," said Catherine, earnestly. She told him the whole story of what her Destiny had put her through and how this gift of silk was supposed to make up for it.

After she finished, the king looked thoughtful. "You can have all this gold, if you would like," he said. "After all, I can always have a new crown made. But if there is anything else you would like that I can give to you, I promise I will."

Catherine thought hard. As she did so, her eye was caught by the king's half-finished garment. It had been so long since she sewed something beautiful, and her fingers itched with longing to embroider dainty designs once more. "What I really love is to sew," she said. "I would like a position at the palace, making beautiful and elegant clothes for you and your new queen."

"Done!" the king beamed.

And so, the golden silk was used to finish the king's outfit, and Catherine moved into the palace. The queen adored the outfits Catherine sewed for her, and Catherine's creations became famous throughout the kingdom.

In her later years, Catherine admitted to herself that although her Destiny had spoiled her younger years, she truly was the happiest old lady in the entire kingdom, for she had spent the rest of her life doing what she loved.

Elisa and the Swans

Based on a traditional German story

A long time ago, in a rich and pleasant land, there lived a princess named Elisa. Her father, the king, was a gentle man, who doted on all of his children since their mother had died. Elisa had eleven older brothers, who all adored their little princess. Despite all their riches, the children were not spoiled. Princess Elisa especially was known for being good and kind.

When Elisa was ten, her father met a new wife. She seemed like a good lady—until after the wedding. She was nice to the king himself, but she was cruel to the children. She didn't like little Elisa's goodness; it made her feel bad about herself. So, she banished Elisa to a cottage in the woods and told the king she had sent her to get the finest education in the country.

Elisa escaped from the cottage as soon as she could and ran back to the palace. When she arrived, she was dismayed to find that her brothers were all gone.

"Don't bother looking for them," said her stepmother at the door. "You will never find them."

"I want to see my father," Elisa demanded.

But the stepmother closed the door in Elisa's face.

Elisa searched the whole kingdom, but nowhere could she find her brothers or anyone who had even seen them.

One afternoon, tired and feeling hopeless, she was walking through a forest near the coast. She bumped into an old lady who was picking raspberries.

"I don't suppose you have seen eleven princes riding in this forest?" Elisa asked.

The old lady looked thoughtful. "Eleven princes, no," she said. "But eleven white swans with tiny golden crowns were flying above the shore near here yesterday."

Eleven of them, Elisa thought to herself. Could it be a coincidence?

She asked the lady to show her to the ocean, which stretched out in front of her like a vast blue plain.

Then, she saw white wings on the horizon. Sure enough, eleven snowy white swans flew into view. They seemed to spot her and flew directly toward her. When they reached her, they circled her from above. Elisa was certain that, somehow, these were her brothers.

"I've missed you!" she called.

The sun was sinking in the sky, and the swans flew lower. As soon as it dipped beneath the horizon, they touched down on the beach next to Elisa and were transformed into humans again.

"We've missed you, too!" they were finally able to say, hugging their sister close.

"Our stepmother put a wicked enchantment on us," scowled Karl, the eldest brother.

"During the day, we become swans, and we must keep flying all the time. Only when the sun sets each evening do we turn back into humans, and then we can rest," said Jens, the fourth brother.

"We live in another land across the sea now," added Hans, the youngest brother.

"We only came back here to search for you. Now we can take you with us."

They spent all night gathering willow bark and rushes and weaving them into a basket to carry Elisa across the sea.

When dawn broke, Elisa settled herself into the net. Her brothers transformed back into swans the second the golden sun rays hit them, and they picked up the basket and took off.

Elisa found herself flying above the ocean, with all eleven of her brothers flapping overhead. It was the strangest and most thrilling experience of her life! The journey was long and difficult, but finally the new land was in sight.

They landed outside a large cave, big enough to shelter them all for the night.

"This is where we usually rest," Hans explained. "It could be a safe home for you."

Elisa nodded, but she wasn't planning on staying in the cave. She was determined to find some answers and free the brothers from their curse. They all huddled together to sleep. Elisa drifted off, still turning the problem around in her head.

She dreamed of a beautiful fairy, with golden hair, who looked strangely like the old lady who had told her about the swans. "You want to lift the curse from your brothers," the fairy said, smiling kindly at Elisa.

"I do," Elisa replied, in the dream. "More than anything."

"There is a way," said the fairy. "But it will require great courage and strength on your part." She held up a stinging nettle. "These grow around the entrance of your cave and in the graveyard nearby. You must pick them, even though they will burn your hands like fire. You must crush them, even though they will hurt your feet like bee stings. Then, you will have flax. You must weave this flax into fine shirts with long sleeves. Once you have made them all, throw them over the swans, and the curse will be lifted."

Elisa nodded eagerly. "I will do it!"

The fairy held up a hand. "There is something else. From the time you start this task to the time you finish, you must not speak a single word to anyone. Not one word, even if it takes you years. If you speak, your brothers will all drop dead. Good luck, little sister."

The fairy leaned forward and brushed Elisa's hand with the nettle she was holding. Elisa woke up, with her hand burning like fire. It was dawn, and as her brothers left the cave and took to the air in their swan forms, Elisa started to pick the nettles near her cave.

The pain was worse than she ever could have imagined. Within minutes, her hands and arms

were covered with itchy, red lumps. Elisa almost cried out in pain several times and was forced to clamp her mouth closed.

Once she had collected as many as she could carry, she took them into the cave and began to crush them with her feet. It hurt worse than a hundred bee stings. Tears welled up in Elisa's eyes and poured down her face, but still she didn't utter a peep.

Next, it was time to spin the flax. Without a spinning wheel, she had to do it all by hand. Although the sting was gone from the nettles now, they were rough and painful on her sore hands. Once she had made some thread, she began to weave it into a shirt.

By the end of the day, as the sun sank low in the sky and her brothers appeared on the horizon, Elisa felt like crying. She had only managed to spin enough flax to weave one cuff.

The princes were dismayed to find their little sister looking sad.

"We thought you would like it in this kingdom," said Hans. "What's wrong?"

But Elisa couldn't tell them, and the brothers were saddened that she didn't seem to like their new home.

Day after day, Elisa continued her task, pushing through the pain and thinking only of the love for her brothers.

One day, when she had almost made all of the shirts, she saw that she had used up all of the nettles from around the cave, and she was forced to venture into the graveyard. Once she had gathered armfuls of nettles, she was spotted leaving the graveyard by some of the people from the nearby town.

"Why, she is gathering plants from the graves of the dead!" cried one of them in disgust. "Only witches and ghouls do such things! She must be collecting horrid materials for her potions and spells."

"We must destroy her before she harms us!" cried another.

An angry crowd gathered outside the cave, holding burning torches, to capture the witch. Elisa heard the angry shouts approaching and worked even harder. She was so close to finishing her task.

From high in the sky, her brothers heard the

commotion and swooped down to the cave to protect their little sister.

Elisa saw them coming and threw the shirts over them. They were instantly transformed back into human princes. Hans was left with one swan wing instead of an arm, since the sleeve of the last shirt hadn't been finished.

"I can speak! I'm not a witch!" Elisa cried.

Together, she and her brothers told the story of their wicked stepmother and what she had done to them all.

The people of the kingdom were astonished, and they all felt bad for suspecting Elisa of being an evil witch, when she had been fighting against evil alone for so long. They told the young princes and princess that they were all welcome to stay for as long as they wanted.

The brothers gathered around to hug their little sister.

"Oh, Hans," said Elisa, with tears in her eyes. "I'm so sorry I didn't finish the final sleeve. Now you will have a wing forever."

Hans hugged her close with one arm and one wing. "I'm not sorry," he said. "Now we will all be reminded forever of what you did for us, little sister. My wing is a sign of your bravery and strength for all to see."

How the Moon Was Made

Based on Maori myths

A long time ago, in the land of Aotearoa, lived two young girls, named Marama and Hana. They were both very curious and loved to explore. They would spend all day roaming the land, looking for interesting things. When night fell, their hearts would sink, for in those days, there was no moon in the sky. The bright, burning sun lit the daytime, and the night was full of darkness and shadows. The girls had no choice but to go home and wait until first light to start their adventures again.

One day, Marama came running to find Hana. "I've just heard of the most amazing thing!" she cried. "Deep in the underworld is a fire that never goes out! It's guarded by fierce spirits, but if anyone can capture it, they will be able to live forever. What a prize that would be. And what an adventure! Will you come with me to find it?"

"How would we find our way to the underworld, though?" Hana asked. "Surely only the dead can pass that way?"

"We will take the Spirits' Pathway," Marama announced, confidently.

Hana gasped. "Living people cannot walk that way!"

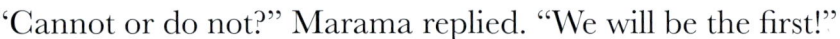

Everyone in Aotearoa knew that the spirits of the dead all journeyed to a place named Cape Reinga. There, they would leap off the headland. Halfway down, jutting out from the rocky slope, was a pohutukawa tree with crimson flowers and twisting roots. The spirits would land in the tree and climb down through the tangle of roots and into the hole in the ground beneath them. This was the entrance to the underworld.

"Cannot or do not?" Marama replied. "We will be the first!"

And so, the two girls prepared for the long journey to the northernmost tip of Aotearoa. They packed provisions for themselves and a basket of delicious sweet potatoes to distract the spirits with. As they waved goodbye to their families, they pretended they were just visiting the next town, for they didn't want their parents to worry.

It was a hard journey. It was as if the entire Earth knew the terrible danger that the girls were about to put themselves in and was trying to head them off. Trees pulled at their clothes, and the wind blew back against them. Wild animals stood in their way, and even the mountains themselves grew a little taller in the hope that the struggle of the journey would make the girls give up and turn back.

But nothing would dissuade them.

"This is the greatest adventure we have ever had!" Marama exclaimed.

"Yes, we have seen so much," Hana agreed.

Finally, after many, many days, the girls reached the end of the land at Cape Reinga. Standing high on the headland, with the wind whipping around them and the waves crashing on the rocks below, they both felt truly scared for the first time.

Hana peered over the edge of the cliff to spot the pohutukawa tree. It suddenly looked very far away, and the rocks beneath were jagged and rough.

"Just think," said Marama. "If we are successful, this is the only time we will ever have to do this jump. Once we have the fire, we will live forever."

Hana nodded.

They held hands tight and leaped down toward the tree. Hana felt the urge to scream as she plummeted, but she didn't want the spirits to hear her. A few moments later, they landed safely in the scratchy branches.

Marama scrambled down the trunk first. She spotted the hole beneath the roots, just narrow enough to slip through and darker than the night, though she could see flames coming from deep within. Marama took a deep breath, as if she was about to dive beneath the surface of a lake, and leaped in.

Hana, watching from behind, saw her friend disappear completely into what looked like the mouth of the Earth. Her courage almost failed her, but she knew that even if the worst horrors of the underworld awaited her, she could never leave Marama to face them alone. So, she threw the basket of sweet potatoes through the hole and then slipped into the tree herself.

After a moment, their eyes adjusted to the dim light and they found themselves in a long, stone passageway leading deeper underground. Silently and carefully, they began to walk.

Sometimes, the hair on the back of Hana's neck would prickle, and she wondered if a spirit was about to pass them by on the way to the underworld. But if it did, she couldn't see it.

After a long time, they saw a light gleaming up ahead. They crept even more quietly now, placing their feet slowly and softly on the rocky floor.

Marama took the lead as they approached the end of the passageway and the space beyond, where the light was coming from. She flattened herself to the wall and then cautiously peered through the doorway.

Ahead was what looked like a grassy plain, like the plains above the ground. In the middle of it, a fire was burning. It was built from only three crossed sticks, but it was blazing more brightly and fiercely than the biggest bonfire they had ever seen.

"There it is!" Marama breathed. "The fire that never goes out!"

Hana felt quite dazzled by the dancing flames after walking in the dark for so long. "It's beautiful!"

Their attention shifted to the figures sitting around the fire. They had human form, and they all appeared to be of a great age, with silver hair and lined faces.

"They don't look fierce," Hana whispered, hopefully.

"That's because they don't know we are here yet," Marama replied. "Pass me the basket of sweet potatoes."

Hana did as she said.

"Now, let us be brave," said Marama.

She marched into the cavern, holding the basket up high. "Hello," she began.

The spirits all sprang to their feet, with hisses of alarm.

"Who are you?" demanded one.

"They are alive!" cried another.

"Living mortals in the underworld. We cannot allow this!" cried the third. "Something has gone terribly wrong!"

They began to march toward the girls.

"No, you don't understand," Marama said, fighting to keep her voice steady. "We

just came to bring you this lovely food. We know you must miss it, here in the underworld."

The spirits' eyes gleamed as they saw the sweet potatoes in the basket.

"It has been so long since I tasted that goodness," one of them muttered.

Marama placed the basket on the ground and gestured to it. The spirits approached, eagerly, like birds flocking to dropped grain.

As soon as she saw that they were distracted, Marama ran to the fire, grabbed one of the sticks, and she and Hana ran back toward the tunnel, as quickly as they could.

But a moment later, a loud screech of rage sounded behind them. "You tricked us!"

Hana glanced behind to see that the spirits had tipped over the basket in their rage and were flying through the air toward them.

"Quickly, quickly!" she called to Marama.

They bolted into the tunnel, Hana in the lead and Marama right behind her, still clutching the burning stick. They ran faster than they had ever run in their lives. Up ahead, they could see the entrance lit by the rosy glow of the setting sun.

"Almost there!" Hana cried, but even as she did so, she heard the spirits right behind them.

Hana scrambled up through the hole first.

As Marama went to follow her, she felt a cold hand close on her heel.

"They've got my foot!" she shrieked.

Hana immediately grabbed Marama's free hand and tried to haul her up above ground, but the spirits had a firm grip on her foot.

"Give us back our fire!" they snarled.

"No!" Marama kicked her foot, but she couldn't dislodge them. She worried that they were about to pull her—and the fire—back into the underworld. "The fire is ours now, you will never get it back!" she yelled. Then, she hurled it up into the sky with all her might, and it stayed hanging up there, high above the Earth.

Hana pulled both of Marama's hands and dragged her back up onto the land.

The spirits were too afraid to come above ground, and they retreated, growling and cursing the girls.

"All that effort, and we lost the fire," Marama grumbled.

"I don't suppose we will get everlasting life with it stuck all the way up there," Hana agreed, gloomily.

The sun sank against the horizon, taking the last of its golden rays with it. But to the girls' surprise, they were not plunged into the darkness of night. High up above, the fire still burned brightly with a silvery light, illuminating the land all around them.

"We might not have everlasting life, but now we can see at night!" Hana exclaimed. "Well done, Marama!"

This is how the Moon came to be. And so, the girls started the long journey home, and looked forward to all the new adventures they hoped to have.

Iara and Her Brothers

Based on a tale from the Tupi people of Brazil

A long time ago, in the rain forests of Brazil, there lived a young girl named Iara. She was the daughter of the chief of her tribe. Everybody loved Iara—it was impossible not to! She was clever, funny, kind, and determined. When she grew up, she also became a fierce and strong warrior, the best in all the tribe.

"My daughter, you are such a blessing to me," her father said to her one day. "Everyone knows you are the most fearsome person in the forest. Maybe we should make you the chief one day!"

Iara thought her father was joking. "The chief is always a man!" she pointed out.

"Yes, but the best warrior of the tribe is always a man—until now!" said her father. "You can outrun and outfight them all!"

Iara had two older brothers. They overheard their father praising Iara, and they were overcome with jealousy.

"How dare he say Iara should be chief!" spat the older one. "I should be chief when the time comes."

"And we are better warriors than her," grumbled the younger one, even though in their hearts they both knew that was not true.

The more they saw their father and the other members of the tribe praising Iara, the angrier they became.

"We need to put a stop to this once and for all," said the older brother, grimly.

"How?" asked the younger.

"Iara must die," said the older one.

The younger brother was shocked. "But she's our sister!"

"Exactly," said the older one. "She is our sister. Only a girl, and she shines brighter than both of us put together. Do you want to live your whole life being thought of as worse than a girl?"

"No," the younger one decided. "Very well, we must kill her. But how? She could beat each of us in a fight."

"I know," agreed the older brother, although it was painful for him to admit it. "I believe she could beat both of us if we attacked her together, as well."

The younger brother threw up his hands. "So how shall we manage it?" he asked.

The older brother's eyes glimmered. "All warriors are vulnerable sometimes. Do you think Iara will be able to fight us if she is asleep?"

The younger brother felt very nervous about the plan. He knew how cowardly it was to kill a warrior while they slept, but he agreed with his brother; it was the only way they could defeat Iara.

They waited until a dark night when there was no moonlight. That evening, they waited for the rest of the tribe to go to bed, and then longer still to make sure that everyone was fast asleep.

Iara was still sleeping soundly as they tiptoed toward her bed, holding on tight to their weapons.

The brothers stood over their little sister, and on a silent signal from the elder brother, they both attacked, one with a stick and the other with a spear. But in that moment, Iara's eyes snapped open, and she rolled out of the way, springing to her feet.

"Brothers, what are you doing?" she demanded, her eyes open wide.

"You are not better than us," snarled her older brother, stabbing furiously.

Iara dodged every blow. She was much nimbler than both of her brothers. "Please stop! What have I done to hurt you?"

"You have stolen our father's love and made us look like fools in front of the whole tribe," hissed the younger brother, aiming a hard blow at her legs with his stick.

Again and again, they attacked. Iara dodged them. She didn't want to attack her brothers back, and she didn't call for help; she knew that they wouldn't be able to hurt her, and she didn't want to cause her father to worry in front of the rest of the tribe.

"Just give up!" Iara pleaded with them, leaping out of the way of another swipe. "You aren't going to be able to kill me, and if you leave me alone, I won't tell Father what you tried to do just now."

"Ha, as if we can trust a woman," said the eldest brother, sweating as he attacked Iara ever more viciously.

Iara felt truly angry then. "I can be trusted as a woman and a brave warrior," she said, acidly. "The only people who can't be trusted are you cowards."

Her words stung her brothers, for they knew they were true. They felt angrier than ever and attacked even more furiously.

Iara grabbed the weapon right out of her younger brother's hands and turned it upon him as he charged her. He ran straight into it and fell to the ground. The older brother gave a shout of fury and threw his spear at Iara's heart. She caught it and dealt him a blow to the head that was so hard that he fell down.

Iara knew that they were both dead, and torches began to flare in the darkness of the night. Others in the tribe had heard the final commotion and came to investigate.

Iara's father arrived first. He gasped with horror when he saw his dead sons and then bellowed in anger to see Iara standing over them. "Iara, what have you done?" he cried.

"I didn't—" Iara began, feeling panic welling in her heart. "I mean they—I tried—Father, they tried to kill me!"

"Why would they do that?" her father demanded.

"They said they were jealous, that I'd made them look like fools," Iara sobbed.

Her father folded his arms. "I don't believe you. Your brothers would protect you, always. Your wild warrior abilities have made you monstrous! You will pay for this, Iara!"

Before he could grab her, Iara leaped around him and ran away into the night. Behind her, she could hear her father telling the whole tribe that she was a murderer.

"She took the lives of my two sons, and now she must pay for that with her own life!" her father yelled.

Iara raced away through the trees as she heard the pounding footsteps and yells of her tribe racing after her. It was a horrible feeling to turn from being so praised and beloved to being chased and hated.

Iara ducked under vines, leaped over twisted roots, and splashed through streams. No matter how fast or far she ran, the tribe was never going to give up and leave her alone.

For what felt like hours, she dodged and dived, zigzagging through the forest. Eventually, Iara began to tire, and her sharp warrior senses were dulled. To her shock, she rounded a huge tree trunk to find some of the men of her tribe standing before her, blocking the way. She turned to run back the way she had come, but there were more men behind her, including her father.

"This is wrong!" Iara cried. "My brothers attacked me!"

But nobody would listen to her. Her father gave the order that her punishment was death by drowning. The men of the tribe bound Iara's arms to her sides and dragged her to the river. Two of them waded into the water and pushed Iara's head down beneath the surface.

To Iara's surprise, as she struggled against her captors, several little silvery blue fish swam up to her.

"Iara, it's Iara! The most fearsome warrior of the forest!" one of the fish said, in a high-pitched, bubbly voice.

"Your tribe are fools, and they don't deserve you!" squeaked a second.

"You can live with us, where we will value you," suggested a third.

Iara was so astonished to hear the fish talking that she gasped and took a big gulp of water by accident! She began to splutter.

"Let go of the air, Iara," said the fish. "You don't need it anymore."

The fish began to swim around in a circular pattern, saying, "Join the water, Iara. Join the water, Iara."

Iara felt dizzy and heavy, and everything went dark.

When Iara woke, she was still face down in the water, but the dizziness was gone. Nobody was holding her limbs or her head now, and she couldn't hear any shouts from the surface. Instinctively, Iara went to lift her head to take a breath of air. But as she was about to, she sensed she was already breathing—underwater!

The same silvery blue fish from before appeared in front of her. "Iara, you are awake. Queen Iara is awake!"

"Queen Iara?" Iara repeated. "How can that be? What has happened to me?"

One of the fish swam right up to Iara. "Your tribe tried to kill you. They think they succeeded, but we saved you with our river magic. Do you like your tail?"

With astonishment, Iara looked down to see that her legs had transformed into a shimmering golden tail. "I'm a mermaid!" she gasped.

"We hope you will be happy living in the river with us," said the fish.

Iara found that she was indeed very happy in the river. She rode the currents with the fish, explored the forests of underwater plants, and met all of the other river creatures. Sometimes she would play in the rapids; other times, she would bask in the calm, sun-warmed shallows of remote riverbanks.

But although Iara enjoyed her new life, she never forgot what the men of her tribe had tried to do to her. If she ever saw any of them in the forest, she would always take her revenge. She would sit on the riverbank and call them over. Fascinated by seeing a mermaid, the men would approach, and once they were close enough, Iara would pull them into the river and drown them, exactly as they had tried to do to her.

And just as they had before, whenever anyone spoke of Iara, they called her the most fearsome person in the forest.

The Green Serpent

Based on a French tale

A long time ago, in a kingdom of magic and spells, lived a king and queen. The royal couple were blessed by great happiness when the queen gave birth to twin girls. They named them Bellotte and Laidronette.

They invited all the fairies of the kingdom to a wonderful feast to celebrate the two new princesses. It was the custom for fairies to give magical gifts to all royal babies. The fairies all cooed over the sweet newborns, but as they were sitting down to eat, the door of the banqueting hall banged open. On the threshold was Magotine the fairy. The king and queen shuddered. They hadn't invited Magotine on purpose because she was evil and cruel.

"Am I not good enough to meet the new princesses?" croaked Magotine.

"It was a mistake!" cried the king, fearing that Magotine would harm the babies.

"An oversight," the queen added. "We are so sorry Magotine. Please, let me set you a place at the table."

But Magotine would not accept their apology. She waved her wand, and everything on the table turned to snakes.

There was chaos as all the fairies at the table leaped up to get away from the hissing, writhing serpents. In the confusion, Magotine slipped over to the cradles, where the two princesses were napping.

She leaned over the side of Laidronette's crib, prodded the princess with her wand, and said, "My gift to you is that you will be the ugliest creature ever to exist!"

Laidronette began to cry.

Magotine turned to put a similar curse on Bellotte, but the other fairies heard Laidronette crying and came rushing over.

"Leave the princesses alone!" cried one of them.

Magotine fled from the cribs and jumped straight through a window.

As the princesses grew up, Bellotte became incredibly beautiful and charming. Laidronette was extremely intelligent, but her ugliness grew year after year, until even her own family could hardly bear to look at her.

Laidronette hated the way that even her own family flinched at the sight of her, so when she was twelve, she asked to go and live in a castle by herself, deep in the forest.

Life in the forest was lonely, but Laidronette found it bearable. She read lots of books, took many walks among the beautiful trees, and she painted, wrote, and sang.

One day, when she was walking through the forest, she was alarmed to come across an enormous green serpent curled up under a tree. Fearing that the monster might attack, Laidronette tried to creep past as quietly as possible. But as she tiptoed, the serpent lifted its head and said in a deep voice. "Laidronette, you are not alone. I was born even more beautiful than you, and look what happened to me!"

Laidronette shrieked with alarm and ran away as fast as she could. She ended up on a beach that she had never seen before. Bobbing in the shallows was a beautiful golden boat. Laidronette was curious to see the inside of such a pretty boat, so she climbed on board.

The instant her feet touched the deck, the wind whipped up, and the boat was swept out to sea on towering waves. Laidronette was terrified as she clung to the mast. Soon, she was in the middle of a stormy sea, with no land in sight.

"Laidronette, I can help you," came a comforting voice. "Hold on to me, and I can swim you to shore."

Laidronette looked down into the water and saw that it was the Green Serpent who had spoken. She screamed in fright. "Get away from me, you horrid beast!"

"I wish you could see my true nature," the Serpent replied sadly, as he swam away. "I only look beastly in the way that you look ugly. It isn't real."

The boat was dashed against some rocks and fell to pieces. Laidronette climbed onto the rocks, soaked and shivering. "What a sad end to my sad life!" she wailed.

She curled up on the rock, crying and feeling hopeless because she knew nobody would find her this far out at sea. After a while, she drifted off into a miserable sleep.

To her surprise, when she woke up, she was in a warm, comfortable palace, with beautiful paintings on the wall, stunning gardens, and fountains outside. Servants bustled in to attend to her every need, and none of them flinched when they saw her face.

Laidronette quickly checked in a mirror and saw that she was still as ugly as ever.

"Please, how did I get here?" she asked.

"Our master, the Invisible King, brought you here," said the servants. "He wishes you to stay as his friend."

"How kind!" Laidronette cried. "May I meet your king to thank him in person?"

The servants shook their heads. "Alas, nobody is allowed to gaze upon him for seven years. You can speak through a curtain, if you wish."

Laidronette was taken to a room with a long purple curtain hanging down the middle of it. She sat on one side.

From the other side came a friendly voice. "Hello, Princess Laidronette. You are welcome to my kingdom."

"Thank you! I've never had a friend I couldn't see," Laidronette said. "Although," she added, "it might be better that you can't see me. I'm the ugliest creature alive."

"I disagree!" said the voice. "You might not be able to see me, but I have seen you. I see your goodness, kindness, and intelligence. I know that you have been cursed. I have, too, and if anyone looks at me, my seven years of penance starts all over again."

"Did Magotine do that to you, too?" asked Laidronette.

"Who else?" replied the voice, bitterly. "But she shall not ruin our lives. This lovely palace is ours, and I think we are going to be the best of friends!"

And it seemed that the Invisible King was right. He and Laidronette got along splendidly. They listened to music together, discussed books, and shared their dreams.

After some time, Laidronette sent word to her family that she was alive and invited them to visit the kingdom. When her parents arrived, they were horrified to hear that Laidronette was living with a friend whom she had never seen.

"He's clearly not a king, he's a monster!" cried the queen.

"And you are not his friend, but his prisoner!" said her father.

Laidronette was stung by their words and sent them home, shouting, "He is under a curse, like I am. None of you know what it is like!"

Still, she began to wonder if she really was the prisoner of a monster. That night,

when the whole palace was asleep, she snuck into the king's bedroom. To her horror, slumbering on the bed lay the Green Serpent!

As Laidronette gasped, the Green Serpent awoke in a panic. "What have you done?" he cried.

Magotine appeared in a flash of lightning. "She has extended your curse!" she cackled. "And got a second curse of her own!"

With a click of her fingers, she sent the Green Serpent into the Underworld to serve seven more years. Laidronette became Magotine's servant, and the evil fairy enjoyed setting cruel tasks for the princess. Poor Laidronette was forced to climb a mountain wearing iron shoes and fill a bucket full of holes with water.

One day, Magotine told Laidronette to go to the Fountain of Life and Wisdom and bring her water from it. She believed it would increase her power.

When Laidronette got there, she was thirsty and hot, so she drank the water and then splashed it on her face. She felt tingly all over, and when she looked into the pool, she saw that she was beautiful once more!

The eldest fairy who had been at her birth celebration all those years ago appeared. "Oh, Laidronette,

you have done it! This water is the only thing that can lift Magotine's curses. If you come with me, I can help you hide from her forever."

Laidronette wanted to run away with the fairy, but she thought of the Green Serpent and how it was her fault he was toiling away in the Underworld for another seven years. "I must help my friend before I hide," she said.

"But Magotine is sure to find you!" the fairy protested.

"Then I will have to face her," Laidronette said. "But it would be wrong to leave someone who was so kind to me."

So, she filled up a bottle with the Water of Life and Wisdom and began the long and dangerous journey into the Underworld. It was a cruel land of sharp rocks, poisonous fumes, and misery. Several times, Laidronette thought she would be captured by the horrible creatures who made their home down there.

At last, she saw the Green Serpent curled up by a rock.

"My friend!" she called. "I am sorry I ever doubted you! I've come to help you, Quick, drink this."

The Green Serpent looked shocked. "Laidronette! Your curse is gone!" he drank the water and at once, he transformed into a very handsome young man.

"You have lifted my curse, too!" he cried. "How can I ever thank you?"

"You don't have to," Laidronette said, with a smile. "You were kind to me, and so now I wish to be kind to you."

At that moment, Magotine appeared, her eyes flashing. "You won't get away from my curses so easily!" she snapped. "I can just put them back on you!"

The wise fairy appeared. "Actually, you can't, Magotine," she replied. "The one thing stronger than your magic is kindness. Now that they have each been kind to one another, their bond of friendship shall protect them and remain unbroken."

Magotine stamped and wailed with fury.

Laidronette and the prince returned to his castle, where they lived in happiness and friendship for the rest of their lives.

The King and His Daughters

Based on a story from northern India

A long time ago, there lived a king with three daughters. The princesses were all close, but they had very different personalities. The eldest, Rani, was brave and steady. She supported her father in all practical ways. The second, Jia, was full of joy. She lit up the whole palace with her laughter and cheer. The youngest, Lakia, was the most thoughtful of the three. She was sweet and kind and made every person who spent time with her feel very special.

The king loved all three of his daughters, but he was an insecure man and he started to wonder which of his daughters loved him the most. He decided that he wanted to test their love for him. He sat in his throne room and sent for Rani. His eldest daughter came into the room.

"What is it you need, Father? May I take a message for you?" Rani offered, as a dutiful daughter.

The king held up a hand. "Not right now, Rani. I actually wanted to ask you a question."

Rani sat at her father's feet. "What is it, Father?"

The king leaned forward in his throne. "How much do you love me?"

Rani thought seriously for a moment. "I love you as much as all the gold and all the silver in the world. The worth of all of it added together is how much I love you, Father. You couldn't be any dearer to me."

The king sat back, smiling. He was pleased that Rani could see his value. "What a lovely reply, my dear. Thank you. Now, will you sit with me while I ask the same question of your sisters?"

Rani took a spot in the throne room.

The king sent for his second daughter, Jia.

"Are you bored, Father?" Jia asked when she entered the room. "I've got some great jokes for you."

The king smiled. "Maybe a little later, my dear Jia. For now, I would only like to ask you a question."

"If it's whether I would like a pony, the answer is yes," joked Jia, with a twinkle in her eyes.

The king chuckled. "You already have five ponies, Jia. No, my question is how much do you love me?"

Even fun-loving Jia could see how seriously her father was taking his question and how anxiously he was waiting for the answer. So, she managed to be solemn for a moment. "I love you like rubies and diamonds," she replied. "You are like the biggest and brightest diamond in the world. Everyone is dazzled by your brilliance, Father."

The king beamed at his second daughter. "You think I am that great?"

"Of course, Father!" said Jia. She was very happy to have pleased him.

The king nodded. "That is good to hear. Please, come and sit with Rani and wait while I ask your sister the same question."

He summoned young Lakia to come to the throne room. As soon as she came in, she frowned slightly. "Father, what is it? You look a little anxious," she said.

The king smiled fondly at his youngest daughter. He was sure he already knew the answer to this question, for she was the most loving and kindly of all his daughters. "Nothing is wrong; I just wish to ask you a question," he explained. "How much do you love me?"

Lakia's eyes widened. She knew right away what an important question she was being asked and she was determined to answer it as best she could. She thought hard and then said, in a strong, clear voice: "I love you like salt."

Her sisters gasped.

The servants standing around the edge of the throne room looked concerned.

The king scowled. "Salt? The most common, worthless substance in all the land? Your sisters love me more than gold, silver, and jewels. And you compare me to salt?"

Lakia spread her hands. "Father, let me explain—" she asked.

But the king's fury was already too great. "I think we've heard quite enough from you," he snapped. "In fact, I never want to hear anything from you again. I have given you everything you could ever want, as one of my precious daughters. And you cannot even love me well in return."

To Lakia's horror, the king ordered for her to be banished from the kingdom, immediately.

Even her sisters didn't speak up for her. They were frightened of their father's fury and worried that he might turn his wrath on them if they protested Lakia's punishment, even if they didn't understand why she had likened her love for the king to salt.

Lakia found herself outside the palace, with only the clothes that she was dressed in. Beyond the palace was a huge forest. Lakia hoped she might be able to find shelter in there, so she set off into the trees.

She walked for days and days. She slept under wide, spreading leaves, on beds of soft moss, under blankets that she had woven from grass and vines. She scooped up clear

river water to drink and ate berries and nuts that she foraged. Although Lakia was a princess, she did not mind living simply. She understood what was important in life, and the only thing that upset her about her current situation was that her father did not love her anymore.

Eventually, Lakia walked so far, she crossed the border into the next kingdom. She hadn't realized how far she had gone, so she was surprised to bump into Prince Atfat, who was out hunting. The prince and princess had known each other since they were very young, and they were firm friends.

"Lakia, what are you doing here?" Prince Atfat asked. Then he noticed her dirty, crumpled clothes and her tangled hair. "What happened to you?"

"My father cast me out," Lakia told him. She explained what the king had asked and how angry he had been when she had spoken. "But he doesn't understand what I meant," she wailed. "I wish I could explain it to him!"

Prince Atfat gave his friend a hug. "Well then, let's make sure you get that chance."

He took Lakia back to his palace, and together they made a plan.

A few days later, Lakia's father was pleased to receive an invitation to a banquet that was being thrown for him by Prince Atfat. "I always did like that boy," he said to himself. He dressed in his finest clothes and journeyed to Prince Atfat's palace with all of his attendants.

Meanwhile, Prince Atfat and Princess Lakia were busy preparing. They instructed the servants to decorate the banqueting hall and to buy the finest ingredients, but they gave all of the kitchen staff the day off. Princess Lakia wanted to prepare every dish herself. She knew all the food her father liked best and exactly how he liked it to be prepared. Lakia smiled to herself as she chopped ingredients and stirred pots. She tasted every dish when it was ready. "Perfect," she said to herself.

When the king arrived, Prince Atfat greeted him warmly and took him into the banqueting hall. Servants began to bring out dishes and placed them before the king. The king saw a dish of lamb, which was the food he liked best. He eagerly took a bite, but to his dismay, it didn't taste as good as it usually did. Next, he tried the potatoes, but they were bland and tasteless. The bread wasn't nice either. The king grimaced, wondering if Prince Atfat meant to insult him by serving him nasty food.

"Are you not enjoying the feast, your majesty?" Prince Atfat asked.

"The food doesn't taste right," the king replied. "Do you have any other dishes?"

Prince Atfat clapped his hands. "Bring the king the spinach dish we have prepared specially!"

It so happened that this particular spinach recipe was another dish that the king was rather fond of, so he really hoped Prince Atfat's cooks hadn't messed it up.

A female servant, wearing a veil, brought out the spinach dish. She presented it to the king.

He took a small bite and tasted the spinach. It was so delicious that he took another, much bigger spoonful, then another. He immediately understood what had been wrong with all of the other dishes he had tasted before. "The other dishes had no salt!" he cried.

"This spinach is salted perfectly. It is wonderful! Please could you bring more salt for the other dishes?" he asked the veiled servant.

The servant reached up and pulled off her veil—to reveal that she was actually Princess Lakia!

The king gasped to see his youngest daughter.

Lakia smiled down at her father. "So, the dishes without salt were not worth having?" she asked him.

"No," the king admitted, looking shamefaced.

Lakia knelt and took his hands in hers. "Father, when I told you I loved you as much as salt, that is what I meant. You make everything better. Life is not worth living without you, my dear father."

The king suddenly understood just how deep Lakia's love for him was, and how much more it meant than the love that either of her sisters had professed.

"My dear, can you ever forgive me?" he asked, beginning to weep. "You have loved me the best all along, and I have treated you terribly."

Lakia gave her father a hug. "Of course I forgive you, Father. I do not wish to be in competition with my sisters. We all love you in the best way we know how."

"You are far better and wiser than I," the king declared.

"Princess Lakia is better and wiser than all of us," Prince Atfat agreed. "I hope you will appreciate her from now on."

"I will," the king promised.

So, Princess Lakia went home with her father again. From that day on, the king did his best to be worthy of the love of all of his daughters.

The Little Sister of the Giants

Based on Brazilian myths

Along time ago, in a town in Brazil, there lived a young girl named Angelita. She was one of the kindest, sweetest souls ever to walk the earth. Her inner goodness was like a light within her, and it couldn't help but shine out. It made everyone who laid eyes on her astonished by her beauty.

Angelita's mother had died when she was very young. Some years later, Angelita's father remarried. Angelita's stepmother was known for being a great beauty herself, but it just wasn't the same as Angelita's golden glow—and the older lady was immediately jealous of her stepdaughter. But Angelita's father always knew just how to reassure his wife. "You are the most beautiful woman in the world," he would tell her. And it was true, for Angelita was still a young girl and not yet a woman.

One winter, Angelita's father got sick and died. Although Angelita was devastated, she did her best to support her stepmother and did lots of chores around the house. Every day, they would walk into town together to buy food.

One day, as they were walking through the main square, one of the market traders

muttered to his friend, "Aren't those two the most beautiful women in town? The stepmother is lovely, but Angelita is even more beautiful than her."

Angelita didn't hear the man, but her stepmother did, and she immediately felt the hard pang of jealousy. Her biggest fear had come true, and she knew that Angelita was more beautiful than she could ever be.

After that day, she wouldn't let Angelita leave the house with her anymore. Angelita had to stay inside, cleaning all day, and when visitors came to the house, the stepmother locked Angelita up in the attic.

A few days later, the stepmother was at the market alone. She heard one of the market traders talking about her again. "Isn't she the most beautiful woman in town?"

The stepmother smiled to herself until a second man answered, "No, her stepdaughter, Angelita, is. She keeps her locked up in the house now, but sometimes you can see Angelita passing by the windows."

The stepmother felt even angrier than she had the first time she had heard such a statement. She marched back home and called her old servant to her. "I want you to take Angelita to the middle of the forest and kill her. I will be the most beautiful woman in the world!"

The old servant's face fell, for he was very fond of little Angelita. "But she's such a sweet girl!" he protested. "How can you want her dead?"

"How dare you question me!" the stepmother snapped. "Do it now, and bring me back the tip of her tongue, so I know that you did."

The old servant quaked as he nodded and went to fetch Angelita.

Angelita thought it was a lovely idea to go for a walk in the forest and thanked the old servant for inviting her. Together, they walked through the trees. But the farther they went, the more distraught the old servant became. Soon, he could not disguise the tears falling down his face.

"Whatever is wrong?" Angelita asked him.

The old servant confessed everything that her stepmother had asked him to do. "But I just can't do it!" he finished. "I could never kill you, Angelita. But you cannot

return home with me. If I don't kill you, your stepmother will just find another way. You must stay in the forest. I will go home and tell her that you are dead."

And so, the old servant went back. On the way back through the forest, he found a fox that had recently died. He cut off the tip of its tongue to take back to the stepmother. She believed the lie, and the old servant breathed a sigh of relief.

Meanwhile, Angelita was wandering the forest alone. She passed lots of animals but no people. After she had walked quite a long way, she came across a huge house in the clearing. The door was twice as tall as her father's entire house, and it had been left standing open. No noise came from inside.

Angelita crept toward the house and stuck her head inside the door. She was met with a mess! A huge stove had been left splashed with various sauces. There were dirty plates and cups scattered on a big long table. There were shelves covered in a layer of dust. Stairs led up to a second level, and, judging from the grimy handrail, the upstairs wasn't any cleaner.

"Hello?" Angelita called. Her voice echoed around the house, and there was no reply. Angelita was so used to cleaning and tidying at home, her fingers itched to clean up the place. "If it is abandoned, I could live here, I suppose," she said to herself. "Even if it is a little big for just one person!"

Angelita set about cleaning the house, and soon she had it all in order. Every surface was gleaming, and there was a lovely scent of spring flowers in the air from the bouquet she had picked.

Just then, Angelita heard a loud, booming noise. She was terrified and ran to hide in a cupboard underneath the stairs. The booming got louder and louder, and the ground began to shake.

Three giants appeared at the door! One was big, one was medium-sized, and one was small, although the smallest one was bigger than the tallest man who has ever lived.

"Wow! Look at our house!" said the biggest as he stomped through the door.

"It's beautiful!" exclaimed the medium-sized one.

"Who could have done all this cleaning?" the smallest one wondered. "And how can we ever thank them?"

Angelita felt a little braver as she listened to the three giants. They seemed like nice boys—just very big! She crawled out from under the stairs and stood up.

"It was me, Angelita," she said. "I'm sorry for coming into your house without asking. I just had nowhere to go, and when I saw this place, I thought it could do with some cleaning." She told them the story of what had happened to her.

The giants' hearts melted as they heard Angelita's sad tale.

"But of course, you must stay with us!" said the biggest giant.

"I agree," said the medium-sized one. "For as long as you like."

"You shall be our little sister!" cried the smallest one.

Every morning, the giants got up to go hunting, and Angelita took care of the house. She loved her new family dearly and felt happy again.

Angelita became friendly with all the creatures of the forest as well—all except for a sneaky little bird. This little bird didn't like to see anyone happy, so he flew all the way

back to Angelita's stepmother and chirped in her ear. "Your stepdaughter is alive and living with three giants in the forest."

Angelita's stepmother was furious. She knew that she would never be happy while there was someone more beautiful than her in the world. "I will have to kill her myself," she muttered as she hurried to visit the local witch.

The witch gave her a pair of roughly made canvas shoes. "Whoever puts these on will fall into the Sleep of Death," the witch said.

"Perfect," the stepmother said, smiling to herself as she paid the witch and hurried away with the shoes. She walked straight into the forest.

It was noon when the stepmother arrived at the giants' house. The giants were all out hunting, and Angelita was sweeping the doorstep when she saw her stepmother emerging from the trees.

Angelita was shocked and scared to see her stepmother, but before she could run indoors, her stepmother waved and smiled.

"Angelita, my dear! I have seen the error of my ways, and I have missed you so much!" she called.

Angelita stayed where she was. "Really?"

"Really!" her stepmother lied. "And to show you how sorry I am, I have brought you a present." She held up the shoes.

"Oh, my!" Angelita cried. "They look exactly like the ones Father made for me when I was little."

"Yes, that's why I got them for you," her stepmother lied again. "Go on, put them on!"

"Thank you, stepmother!" Angelita slipped on the pretty shoes and immediately fell into the Sleep of Death. Her skin was cold, and she did not breathe. Her stepmother ran back home, laughing to herself over how easy it had been to trick Angelita.

When the giants returned home, they were devastated to find Angelita's lifeless body. They knew they couldn't take her to town to bury her, since they would scare everyone. So, they built her a special silver casket and carried it to the nearest pathway through the forest. They left Angelita there for someone to find, and hid to watch.

After some time, a young woman and her little sister came walking through the forest. They were puzzled by the silver casket and stopped to look inside. They were dazzled by Angelita's beauty, even in death.

"She looks like an angel!" the little sister exclaimed. But then she wrinkled her nose. "But those shoes are ugly."

Before the elder sister could stop her, the little sister had reached into the casket and pulled the shoes off.

Immediately, breath and warmth flooded back into Angelita's body. Her eyes snapped open, and she sat up, completely alive once more.

The two sisters screamed but quickly calmed down when Angelita explained her story to them.

The giants came out of their hiding place, sobbing tears of joy to have their dear little sister back.

All four of them went back to their house, where they lived happily ever after, and the two sisters visited them often.

Timun Mas

Based on a traditional Javanese tale

Once upon a time, on the island of Java, there lived a poor widow named Mbok Srini. She lived all alone, since she had no children. Each night, she would sit in her little house on the edge of the jungle, listening to the calls of the wild animals or the rain pattering down on the leaves, and wish she had a child to share her life with. She prayed to every god she knew, asking them to send her a child.

One night, she fell asleep right after she prayed. She dreamed she was walking through the jungle at dawn. She was being drawn to a special spot. She wasn't sure what she would find there, but she was certain that every step was taking her closer to her destiny. She emerged in a clearing full of flowers. At the base of one of the trees sat a little bundle, wrapped in a cloth. Even though Mbok Srini couldn't see a face, she was certain it was a baby.

She awoke from her dream just as the sun was rising.

"It must have been a sign," she said to herself. In a hurry, she dressed and left her house, walking into the jungle at dawn, just as she had in her dream. She felt the same

sense of being drawn to a certain spot. And when she reached the clearing, she saw the same bundle. Mbok Srini fell to her knees, sure that the gods had answered all of her prayers.

Rising again, she hurried to the bundle, but to her surprise, when she picked it up, there was no baby in there at all. In fact, it was empty except for a tiny cucumber seed.

Mbok Srini jumped as she heard a low, menacing chuckle coming from behind her. She turned to see the monstrous green-skinned giant of the jungle, Butho Ijo, watching her.

"I know what you have dreamed of," Butho Ijo said. "And so, I give you this gift." He gestured at the seed in Mbok Srini's hand. "If you plant this seed," Butho Ijo continued, "it will grow into a large cucumber. Inside will be the baby you wish for."

"Oh, thank you!" Mbok Srini cried.

Butho Ijo held up a hand. "I have not finished. You may ask me for more seeds, and more children will grow—but you must give me the first one back once it has grown up."

"What would you want with my child?" Mbok Srini asked, nervously.

"I will not tell you why I must take the child before you agree, but if you do not agree, I shall not give you any cucumber seeds at all," the giant grinned, showing her terrible glistening fangs.

Mbok Srini was wary, but she was so desperate for children that she agreed to this terrible bargain.

She hurried home with the seed and planted it outside her house. She took great care of it, making sure it had enough water, light, and shade. Within a couple of days, the seed sprouted. Soon, a great cucumber grew. When it was ready to pick, Mbok Srini plucked it from the stalk and gently opened it up. Inside was a beautiful, tiny baby girl.

Mbok Srini hugged her close. "My dear, you are here at last!" she crooned. "I will name you 'Timun Mas'." For that name meant "Golden Cucumber."

Although Timun Mas started out much smaller than any other baby, she quickly grew. Under the care and attention of her mother, she grew up into a sweet and loving child. Mbok Srini was so happy and content with her daughter that she soon forgot her promise to give her up to Butho Ijo when she was grown up.

There never was a happier mother and daughter.

When Timun Mas asked why she didn't have a father, Mbok Srini would hug her close and say, "Because you were sent to me by the gods."

"I never want to leave home. Not even when I'm grown up," Timun Mas told Mbok Srini.

But a week before Timun Mas was due to turn seventeen, she went to the village to fetch some food. While she was gone, Butho Ijo appeared outside the family house. "Mbok Srini!" he called. "Will you need more

cucumber seeds? Next week, your daughter will be coming with me. I'll turn her into a tasty dinner. I've been looking forward to eating human stew for seventeen years."

Mbok Srini gasped in horror, for this was worse than she ever could have imagined. She knew she could never allow Butho Ijo to take her beloved Timun Mas away, no matter how many other cucumber-patch babies she could grow, and she racked her brains to think of a plan. She remembered that there was a wise old hermit who lived on a nearby hilltop.

Once Mbok Srini was sure that Butho Ijo had gone back into the forest, she slipped out of the house and hurried to the hermit's house.

She found the hermit sitting outside.

"Please, sir," Mbok Srini said. "I need your help. Butho Ijo is going to come and take my daughter away to eat her!"

The hermit's eyes widened. "That is terrible indeed! Why would the giant attack an innocent girl?"

Mbok Srini explained the deal and fell to her knees in desperation. "I've heard that you know magic. Can you help me save my daughter?"

The hermit felt sorry for Mbok Srini. He went into his house and emerged a few minutes later, holding four cloth bags. "Inside this first bag," he held it up, "are cucumber seeds. In the second bag are needles. In the third, salt, and in the fourth is shrimp paste. Give these bags to your daughter, and when the giant comes for her, tell her she must run and throw the contents of each bag behind her."

"Thank you," Mbok Srini said. She hurried home. At first, she intended to tell Timun Mas right away about the danger that was waiting for her on her birthday, but she couldn't bring herself to do it. Timun Mas was so looking forward to her birthday and being a grown-up. Mbok Srini tucked the four cloth bags away and told herself it could wait one more week.

The day that Timun Mas had been eagerly awaiting and that Mbok Srini had been dreading eventually arrived. As they arose, Mbok Srini knew she could delay no longer. She ran and grabbed the cloth bags. "Timun Mas, remember how you used to ask how you were brought to me, and I said the gods gave you to me?" Mbok Srini asked, urgently.

"Yes, Mama," Timun Mas smiled, sleepily rubbing her eyes.

"Well, that wasn't exactly true," Mbok Srini gabbled. "In fact, you were actually brought to me by the giant Butho Ijo and—"

At that moment, she was interrupted by a fierce cry from outside. "Mbok Srini, it is I, Butho Ijo, and I'm here to take your daughter away and eat her!"

Timun Mas screamed with fright.

Mbok Srini pressed the cloth bags into her daughter's hands. "Run, and when he chases after you, drop these bags behind you! They are magic from the hermit on the hill!"

Timun Mas fled out of the back door. Within moments, Butho Ijo was chasing her. Just as he was about to catch up to her, Timun Mas opened up the first cloth bag and tipped the cucumber seeds behind her.

A cucumber vine sprang out of the earth and wrapped itself around Butho Ijo's legs. He fell to the ground with a colossal thud, and he roared with anger.

Timun Mas hoped he would be stuck forever, but as she raced away, he ripped the vine in two and jumped back to his feet.

"I was promised a girl to eat!" he yelled.

The second time he caught up, Timun Mas opened the next bag and tipped the needles out behind her. The moment the needles hit the ground, they transformed into a forest of sharp bamboo, with spikes that pierced Butho Ijo and made him bleed.

The giant stumbled, growling with pain, but he was on his feet again a moment later in hot pursuit.

Timun Mas was starting to feel like she would never get away. She opened the third bag and tried to hold onto hope as the salts poured out onto the ground.

They transformed the earth behind her into an ocean! The water tossed and roiled. Butho Ijo was completely caught up in it. Timun Mas hoped that the currents would pull him under, but to her horror, when she glanced back over her shoulder, Butho Ijo was swimming strongly. Moments later, he was hauling himself out onto the shore.

"I'll never give up!" he snarled at her. "I don't care how many magic bags you have!"

But of course, Timun Mas knew that she only had one more bag. She sped up, running faster than she had ever run in her life, but with his long giant legs, Butho Ijo was gaining on her effortlessly.

Timun Mas took a deep breath and emptied out the last bag. When the shrimp paste fell to the ground behind her, it turned the earth to boiling hot, volcanic mud. Butho Ijo ran straight into it and sank. He tried to swim as he had in the sea, but the mud was too thick.

Yelling with fury, Butho Ijo was sucked under the surface of the mud, never to be seen again.

Timun Mas raced home to be reunited with Mbok Srini.

"My child, I am so sorry that I bound you to such a terrible fate!" Mbok Srini cried. She explained the whole story to her shaken daughter.

"Mama, you found a way to give me life," Timun Mas said, hugging her mother. "And you found a way to save me. Thank you. Now we can be together forever."

Leelinau, the Lost Daughter

Based on a story from the Chippewa people of the Great Lakes, North America

A long time ago, on the shores of Lake Superior in North America, there lived a great hunter and his family. All of the family loved to spend time with the other people who lived in their village, except for the middle daughter, Leelinau. Ever since Leelinau was very small, she had preferred to wander in the woods rather than spend time with other people.

The other children thought Leelinau was very strange to choose such a lonely life, but what they didn't see was that Leelinau wasn't alone at all. She felt that every plant and animal in the forest was her friend.

As Leelinau grew up, she disappeared for longer and longer spells, occasionally wandering for days on end, curling up in mossy hollows under trees to sleep. She even began to stray into the Manitowok. This was the forest where all of the magic folk lived. Fairies and wild spirits were said to dwell among the trees, bursting with strange and unknowable powers. Most people were afraid of the Manitowok for this reason, but Leelinau never felt that fear.

She wandered freely, deeper and deeper into those uncharted woods. The magic folk saw the wild spirit in her and welcomed her with open arms. Leelinau began to spend entire days out there, returning with her arms full of rare flowers and interesting leaves.

Leelinau's parents worried about their daughter spending so long out in the woods, but every effort to keep her at home resulted in tears and distress for Leelinau. She didn't want to spend time with the other maidens or young men her age.

As time passed, Leelinau became more familiar with the magic of the forest. She would go there to pray for her father's safe return from hunts. Sometimes she would ask the spirits to bless her with sweet dreams.

Eventually, Leelinau was spending more time in the forest than she was at home. She would rise as soon as the pale dawn broke and slip away to the trees, often not returning until the Sun bid farewell to the Earth for the day with beams of orange and pink.

"I worry about her spending so much time in the Manitowok," Leelinau's mother said to her husband. "What if she has been possessed by an evil spirit?"

"Surely not our gentle Leelinau?" her father said. "But perhaps tomorrow you should follow her to make sure."

So, the next morning, when Leelinau crept outside in the early morning dew, her mother followed at a distance. She trailed Leelinau to a big rock in the forest, which overlooked the lake and was overhung by branches heavy with thick green leaves.

There, Leelinau sat, breathed deeply, and whispered to the spirits all around her. "Dear spirits of the dancing leaves, may my spirit dance with yours. Spirit of the bubbling brook, send me sweet dreams. Spirit of the starry night, show me where the most beautiful flowers dwell, deep in the forest."

"Oh, dear," her mother whispered to herself. "Our Leelinau is dwelling more in this world of strange spirits than she is in our own."

She stole home and told her husband what she had seen.

"We cannot fight this magic openly," Leelinau's father decided. "We must lure Leelinau back to us by reminding her how good it is to be surrounded by other people."

They invited all of the local young people to come and play games near their lodge.

Some of the other children tried to play with Leelinau as they had when they were very little. Leelinau just sat at the door of her lodge and gazed dreamily into the sky.

Next, they tried to play music and sing with her, but Leelinau was distracted, listening to distant melodies on the wind that only she could hear.

Leelinau's parents watched sadly. They felt that they were losing their daughter.

It was autumn. The maize in the fields had ripened into a beautiful gold, and the time had come to pick it. It was traditional for everyone to help with this harvest.

"And you are no different to anyone else," Leelinau's mother said firmly, putting a basket in Leelinau's hands.

"But I want to go to the forest," Leelinau protested.

"You live here, and you eat this food," her mother responded. "So, you have to help gather the harvest. And besides, all your friends are in the fields. You might even have a little bit of fun!"

Leelinau took the basket but muttered rebelliously to herself, "All my friends are in the forest, not here."

It was a merry harvesting party in the field. One of the girls, Niimi, found a red ear of corn.

"Ooh, a red ear means a brave admirer will reveal himself soon!" cried one of the other girls. "How lucky for you, Niimi!"

Niimi beamed. "I'm looking forward to getting married and having a lodge of my own, with a family," she said. "Aren't you, Leelinau?"

Leelinau felt a sinking feeling in her stomach. She couldn't think of anything worse. She didn't want to be tied to a lodge, trapped in the loud, busy bustle of daily life. She wanted to be free to wander, to listen to the Earth, to think quietly by herself.

"I hope you get everything you wish for, Niimi," she said, politely. "I don't think my dreams are quite the same."

The other young people exchanged worried glances. They knew what Leelinau's parents feared—that she would be lost forever to the forest.

One of the boys, a mischievous young man named Bineshii, saw that Leelinau had picked an ear of corn that was all bent and crooked. "Hey, do you guys know what a bent piece of corn means?" Bineshii cried, plucking the corn out of Leelinau's basket. "It means that your suitor will be a crooked thief, Leelinau!"

Bineshii only meant to tease, to draw Leelinau into the game, but she simply took the corn back, glanced at it absentmindedly, and then wandered out of the picking field.

Something was becoming clearer to Leelinau. She didn't want to be an outsider forever. She didn't seek solitude; she sought other spirits like her, and they were all to be found in the forest. But she knew that while she had one foot in her human life, she would always be expected to conform to human ways. "Please, spirits, won't you help me?" Leelinau begged. But for once, the forest seemed only to answer her with silence.

The next day, the son of the chief came to Leelinau's parents and asked for permission to marry their daughter. Leelinau's parents were thrilled; they had been worried that nobody would want to marry Leelinau, since she was so different to all the other girls.

But when they told Leelinau of the match, she folded her arms. "I absolutely will not marry him."

"Yes, you will," said her father, with equal firmness. "You will meet him and be polite to him and marry him. He's the son of the chief! We've already set the date."

"And I am the daughter of the greatest hunter," Leelinau retorted. "And I will not marry him."

She ran out of the house and into the woods. "Please, spirits! Don't you see?"

To her surprise, a voice answered her. It was as sweet and mysterious as the breeze. "Yes, sweet Leelinau, we do see. You wish to leave the world of humans, with their false and cruel ways and their lives of dirt and toil. You want to wander the woods with the other free spirits, don't you?"

"Yes, that is what I wish—more than anything," Leelinau said, with a tear in her eye.

"Well then, that is what shall be," the voice replied. "Here you can have a roof over your head, just as fine as your father's in the spreading green branches of the forest. You can sleep just as peacefully as you did there, in air perfumed by flowers. You will be clothed in golden light from the sun, washed by mountain rains, and fed with all the fruits of the forest."

"Who are you?" Leelinau asked, gazing about her.

"I am the Chieftain of the Green Plume," said the voice. "And I hope that we will meet in person one day soon. Consider my offer. There is no rush. The forest will always wait for you."

Leelinau returned home, with a kernel of hope blossoming in her heart.

On the day that her parents had set as the wedding day, Leelinau put on her best clothes

and carefully styled her hair. Then, she went to find her parents. They smiled when they saw her, for they thought she had prepared herself for her wedding.

"Mother, Father," said Leelinau, "I am ready for my new life to begin."

"You will have a very happy life once you are married," said her father.

"No, you don't understand," Leelinau smiled. "I'm not going to get married. I'm going to live in the Manitowok."

Her parents gasped.

"You can't! It's too dangerous!" her mother exclaimed.

"I know our lodge is safe," Leelinau replied. "And I am grateful for my childhood here, but it is not where my future lies. The Chieftain of the Green Plume has invited me to become one of his people, and I know in my heart that this is the right choice for me."

With that, Leelinau hugged her parents and walked calmly away into the forest.

At first, her parents thought that she was just a little bit nervous about her wedding and that she would return home soon, as she always had before. But the sun set and then rose again the next morning, and there was still no sign of Leelinau.

She never returned to the lodge, but Leelinau is happy now that she can be exactly who she always felt she was. She can watch the birds and swim with the fish instead of being tied down to an ordinary life. Fisherfolk out on the wide lake sometimes catch sight of a small figure slipping through the pines, hand in hand with a green-plumed spirit. They smile to see her so happy.

Anush, the Golden Maiden

Based on a traditional Armenian folk tale

Once upon a time in the mountains of Armenia, there lived a kind widower named Daron and his two young children, a lively girl named Anush and a gentle boy named Shen. Anush and Shen's mother had died not long after Shen was born. She had been a very sweet and caring lady, and the whole family missed her enormously.

Some years later, when Anush was ten and Shen was six, Daron met a new lady named Chiva. She had her own daughter, Vanya, who was the same age as Anush. Chiva was very beautiful, and Daron quickly fell in love with her. They were soon married.

Anush and Shen had looked forward to having a stepmother, but to their dismay, Chiva didn't like them at all. She saw them as competition for Vanya, and she wanted them gone. Vanya was a very meek, shy child, and did whatever her mother told her to do.

"We can't afford to feed them," she complained to Daron. "We'd be much better letting them go into the wilderness. Then we can make sure that Vanya gets enough food. It's better to have one healthy child than three weak and sickly ones."

Daron loved his children, but he was a weak-willed man, and after many months Chiva wore him down. One day, he took Anush and Shen on a walk deep into the nearby enchanted forest. It was a warm day, and soon they were all thirsty.

Daron stuck his walking stick in the ground and hung his cloak over it to make some shade for the children. "Sit under this, and I will be back with water soon," he told them.

Anush and Shen did as he said, but he did not return. After several hours, they tried to look for him, but deep in their hearts, they knew that their father had betrayed them and done what Chiva had always wanted.

"Don't worry, Shen," Anush said, giving her brother a hug. "I'm sure we can find the way home. Father will be sorry when he sees us, and he won't turn us away again."

They began to wander through the forest. After a long time, they passed a deep hoofprint from a horse. Rainwater had gathered in the print.

"Anush, I'm thirsty," said Shen. "Can I drink that?"

"No, Shen," said Anush. "Remember, this forest is enchanted and full of strange magic. If you drink from that, you will turn into a horse."

They walked on and soon came to the hoofprint of an ox, also filled with rainwater.

"Please, Anush," Shen begged. "I am so thirsty."

"I am, too, but if you drink that, you will turn into an ox," Anush said. "You must wait until we find some water that is safe."

They walked farther in the baking sun. Next, they found the print of a bear, then the print of a pig, and, finally, the print of a wolf. Each time, Anush kept Shen from drinking the cursed water.

Next, they passed the hoofprint of a lamb. Shen fell to his knees. "I can't keep going! I must drink, Anush!"

Anush nodded her head, sadly. "Very well, you can drink, but you will turn into a lamb, Shen, I'm warning you."

Shen began to scoop the water into his mouth. As soon as it touched his tongue, he was transformed into a lamb. He followed Anush, bleating the whole way as she eventually found the path that led out of the enchanted forest toward home.

When they got home, Daron was out working, so only Chiva and Vanya were there to greet them. Chiva was furious to see Anush again, although she was pleased to see that Shen had been transformed into a lamb.

"At least he is useful now—as an excellent dinner for us," she said, with a nasty grin.

Anush was horrified. She took Shen and fled back into the forest, not stopping until they reached the safety of the mountains.

Once she was sure that Chiva would not be able to find them, Anush stopped running. She sat on a high rock and began to spin the loose pieces of fleece from Shen's

lamb coat, so that she might have something to sell to support them both.

While she was spinning one day, the handheld spindle that she was using slipped from her grasp and fell down through a crack in the rocks.

Anush went to look for it and discovered a little passageway deep into the heart of the mountain. It eventually opened out into a cave, where the spindle lay on the floor. Inside the cave was an ancient fairy. She looked just as shocked to see Anush as Anush was to see her!

"Child, how did you get in here? It is a place of magic that one cannot come to without a reason," said the fairy.

"My spindle fell down, and I was following it," Anush explained.

The fairy frowned. "Tell me, child, are you in a difficult situation?"

Anush confided in the fairy about the troubles she and Shen had had with their wicked stepmother.

The fairy felt great pity for the child before her and secretly decided to test her to see if she was worthy of a fairy gift. "Anush, I have a request to ask of you. I need to take a nap, for I am very tired, but there is an appointment I simply mustn't miss. Please may I lay my head in your lap to sleep? There is a red-hot poker in the fire. When the time comes to wake me, please grab the poker and press it to the bottom of my feet."

Anush was shocked. "But Madam, won't that hurt you terribly?"

The fairy chuckled. "No, my magic protects me. And I sleep such deep, enchanted sleeps, that the heat from the fire is the only thing that will wake me."

Anush nodded. "Very well, I will do it. How will I know the right time to wake you?"

"First, the Blue Fairy will pass through the cave," said the fairy. "You must stay perfectly still and say nothing. Do not wake me. Next, the Red-and-Green Fairy will pass through the cave. When she arrives, that is when you must wake me."

Anush thought that that didn't sound so hard. She settled down in the seat by the fire, with the elderly fairy's head in her lap. Before too long, the soft, rhythmic breath of the sleeping fairy was the only sound in the cave, except for the crackle of the fire and the quiet beat of Anush's own heart.

Anush couldn't tell how much time was passing—it might have been a minute, or it might have been an hour—but suddenly, the Blue Fairy appeared, as if she had just walked through one of the walls. Her hair shimmered with flecks of silver in her rich, jet black hair. It reminded Anush of a starry night sky. The Blue Fairy smiled at her and looked carefully all around the cave.

Anush stayed as still as she possibly could, not even daring to breathe. Eventually, the Blue Fairy seemed to understand that Anush would not be waking the napping fairy. She walked across to the opposite wall and disappeared through it, as if through a doorway.

Anush let out her breath in a rush of relief. A short while later, the Red-and-Green Fairy appeared, lighting up the cave with a festive glow.

Anush immediately pulled the red-hot poker from the fire and pressed it to the sleeping fairy's feet.

"Oof, what is biting me?" the fairy exclaimed as she woke up.

"Nothing, it's the poker. The Red-and-Green Fairy is here," Anush whispered, nervously eyeing the new fairy.

"Excellent," said the older fairy to the Red-and-Green Fairy. "This little one needs our help. Will you give her a gift?"

The Red-and-Green Fairy turned her glowing eyes on Anush. "Would you like riches or fame?"

Anush shifted uncomfortably at this. "Neither, really. I just want to be able to go home and live with my father and brother as we did before. We were not rich before my stepmother arrived, but we were happy."

The Red-and-Green Fairy smiled. "A good answer." She waved her hands and Anush found her clothes transformed into garments of pure gold.

"Thank you!" Anush said, politely.

"Go home," the older fairy advised her. "All will be well."

When Anush climbed out of the cave, she found that Shen was a boy again! Together, they ran home.

When they arrived, Chiva was mightily jealous of Anush's golden clothes. "Vanya should have those!" she exclaimed, forcing Anush to tell her all about the fairies.

Chiva immediately marched to the fairy cave, dragging Vanya with her. The older fairy knew who Chiva was right away, although she said nothing. She offered them both the same test. Chiva was too impatient to wait for the Blue Fairy, so she decided to yell for the Red-and-Green Fairy right away. Vanya also wanted some golden clothes, but she thought it was silly not to follow the older fairy's simple request.

The Red-and-Green Fairy appeared when Chiva called, but she made a different offer than she had extended to Anush. "Would you like the fastest horses in the kingdom or the sharpest sword?"

Chiva was irritated, since she thought they would be offered riches as Anush had been. "A sword may be used to hurt me. And what use is a sword to me if I haven't been trained to wield it? But I am cunning! I choose the horses! Now make my daughter's clothes gold."

"The magic will take effect when you leave the cave," said the fairy, smoothly.

When Chiva and Vanya left the cave, Vanya's clothes were unchanged. Chiva was furious. As she stamped and shouted, a herd of wild horses thundered down the mountain slope and trampled Chiva to death.

Vanya ran home to Daron, Anush, and Shen. She grieved for her mother, but soon came to be grateful for the family she had left. Anush traded her golden clothes for a small herd of goats. Vanya became well known for selling the very tastiest goat cheese for miles around, and they lived together comfortably and happily for many years.

Princess Pyeonggang

Based on a story from South Korea

A long time ago, in the ancient Korean kingdom of Goguryeo, the king and queen welcomed a baby daughter. They rejoiced for their wonderful new princess and named her Pyeonggang. Like all babies, little Pyeonggang cried a lot. Her parents would rock her and comfort her, but it didn't do much good. Pyeonggang cried both day and night.

"This has to get better soon," the queen wailed.

"Why won't you stop crying?" the king moaned as he rocked the unhappy baby.

To their dismay, things did not improve as Pyeonggang grew up. The king and queen found their nerves were frayed to shreds. Over the years of Princess Pyeonggang's early childhood, they tried everything they could think of to get her to stop crying. They tried distracting her with delicious food, but Princess Pyeonggang spat it out and cried. They tried to give her new toys, but Princess Pyeonggang broke them and then cried. They gave her tasty treats, which she enjoyed, but then she cried for more. She became known throughout the kingdom as "The Weeping Princess."

Finally, one day, when Princess Pyeonggang was ten years old, the king reached his wits' end. Princess Pyeonggang had begun to cry because she didn't like the look of the spoon she had been given at dinner. "Princess Pyeonggang, if you don't stop crying this instant, I will marry you to Ondal the Fool when you grow up!" he roared.

Ondal the Fool was a young man who lived in the kingdom. He was a commoner and only fourteen years old himself, but everyone in Goguryeo had heard of this legendarily brainless boy. Ondal was such a foolish boy that he often climbed on his horse the wrong way and ended up riding backward, or he held his sword by the wrong end, and many more silly mistakes besides.

The threat of being married to this man was dire indeed. Princess Pyeonggang's eyes widened and her mouth clamped shut. She didn't make a sound for the rest of the dinner.

The king and queen could barely believe it. They smiled at each other over their plates. Perhaps this threat had finally solved the problem of the weeping princess?

Later that evening, however, when Princess Pyeonggang went to bed, she couldn't find the doll she liked to sleep with, and the crying began again.

The king stormed into her room and once more threatened to marry Princess Pyeonggang to Ondal the Fool. As before, Princess Pyeonggang looked horrified at the prospect. She stopped crying at once and put herself to bed without another bit of fuss.

This cycle continued throughout the years. Every time the princess started to cry, her father

would threaten to marry her off to Ondal, whose legendary foolishness seemed to grow with every change of the season. The princess would stop crying immediately, and everyone in the palace would have some respite.

However, Princess Pyeonggang grew curious about Ondal. She snuck out of the palace to watch him at a distance. At first, she was as amused and astonished as everyone else to see how many silly things Ondal did every day, but as she watched, she saw that there was a lot more to Ondal than many people appreciated.

"He's brave," she said to herself. "No matter how many times he holds the wrong end of the sword and hurts himself, he's never too afraid to draw it and try again."

She watched as Ondal tried to help a little old lady across the street—and inadvertently led her into a puddle of mud. The little old lady was cross and everyone else laughed, but Princess Pyeonggang felt sorry for Ondal, who was covered in mud, too. "He cares about others and tries to help," she said to herself. "I think everyone is too busy laughing at what's on the surface to see what's underneath."

When Princess Pyeonggang came of age, it was time for her to marry. The king wanted her to marry a good prince from another kingdom, so that he could make an alliance. But when he began to present these suitors to Princess Pyeonggang, she folded her arms and shook her head. "I don't want to marry any of these men, father," she said. "You promised me Ondal the Fool. He is the one I will marry."

"Don't be so ridiculous," the king chuckled. "That was just a joke."

"Not to me," said Princess Pyeonggang, stubbornly. "I have grown up intending to marry Ondal. He is the only man for me."

"You cannot marry that fool!" the king shouted.

"You told me you would marry me to the fool if I didn't stop crying!" Pyeonggang folded her arms. "And I cried every day. A king shouldn't break his word!"

The king felt like crying himself when he saw that his daughter meant what she said. "If that's what you want to do, go and do it," he snapped. "I want no part in this."

Princess Pyeonggang walked straight out of the castle and to the house in town where Ondal lived with his mother. She knocked on the door.

Inside, she heard a lady call, "Ondal! Could you answer the door, please?"

"Which one is the door?" came a puzzled response.

"Oh, for goodness' sake, Ondal!" The lady sounded exasperated, and a moment later, the door swung open to reveal a harried-looking middle-aged lady, Ondal's mother. "Hello, how can I—" she trailed off when she saw Princess Pyeonggang and bowed her head with respect. "Your Highness!"

"Hello," Princess Pyeonggang greeted her. "I am here to ask your permission to marry your son. My father has already agreed to the match."

Ondal's mother looked flabbergasted as she opened the door wider to allow Princess Pyeonggang to come in.

"Hello, Ondal," said Princess Pyeonggang. "Would you like to marry me?"

Ondal's eyes grew very wide. "But I'm a fool," he protested.

"Yes, he's the biggest fool in the kingdom," his mother protested.

Princess Pyeonggang smiled. "Maybe he is, but my father promised me since I was little that I could marry Ondal the Fool, and that is what I would like to do."

"Very well, I accept. Does that make me a princess, too?" Ondal asked.

"No, you simpleton!" his mother snapped. She turned to Princess Pyeonggang. "I don't know why you are set on marrying my son, but I thank you for taking this fool off my hands."

And so Princess Pyeonggang and Ondal the Fool were married.

"I am so happy you chose me to be your husband," Ondal said to his new wife. "Although I fear my foolishness will shame you and make your life worse."

"On the contrary," said Princess Pyeonggang. "Foolishness can be helped, but you can't change a man's character. You are brave and kind. Everything else, I can help you with."

Before leaving the palace, Princess Pyeonggang had gathered up all of her fine jewels. Now, she sold them for a large profit, which made her enough money to build a good house for her and Ondal. With the rest of the money, she bought Ondal new weapons and a fast horse.

"I am going to be queen of this kingdom one day, and you will have to help me protect it," Princess Pyeonggang told Ondal.

Every day, she took him riding, until he could ride as well as any person in the land. Next, she taught him archery. Ondal shot arrow after arrow, and when he could hit a target from a hundred paces, Princess Pyeonggang commanded him to join the army.

The king could hardly believe his eyes when the new recruits marched into his palace courtyard for their first day of training, and Ondal was among them. Everyone expected Ondal to drop his sword, or trip and fall, but he performed all the drills perfectly.

"Maybe he's not such a fool after all," the king mused. "And maybe my daughter is a very clever woman!"

Under Princess Pyeonggang's tutoring, Ondal became a well-respected general. One day, the king heard that a huge army was gathering a short way from the palace, intending to take over the kingdom. Princess Pyeonggang saw the army in the distance, and fear gripped her. The invaders looked terrifying.

She found Ondal. "When I married you, I told you I would need you to protect the kingdom one day. I'm afraid that day has come sooner than I planned. It's an enormous army, and the odds of winning are not great. Will you still fight for the kingdom?"

Ondal bowed and replied, "I will not pretend that I am not afraid, but you saw potential in me when nobody else did, so I would gladly march into battle for you."

Princess Pyeonggang ran home to fetch Ondal's weapons as the invading army approached the town. Ondal rallied the people of the town to defend themselves. Armed with ordinary pitchforks, fire pokers, and kitchen knives, they lined up and waited bravely for the invaders.

The invading army was being paid a great deal by the emperor who wished to conquer Goguryeo. They laughed at the townsfolk and drew their swords. They expected an easy fight.

"Come on, everyone! We can defeat these rats!" Ondal cried. But the townspeople were too afraid, and they cowered back. With a roar of fury, Ondal charged at the invaders and began to fight furiously. Even though he was just one person, all the training that Princess Pyeonggang had given him had made him a fearsome fighter.

Within a few minutes, he'd disarmed dozens of soldiers. The invaders were starting to feel nervous. Nobody wanted to be the next one to face Ondal. His bravery gave the townsfolk courage, and they began to fight in earnest. In the end, the soldiers of the invading army decided that they weren't being paid enough to face such a terrifying warrior, and they turned tail and ran.

"Three cheers for Ondal the Fierce!" everyone cried.

"And three cheers for Princess Pyeonggang!" Ondal added. "For it is truly she who saved the kingdom!"

Savitri's Love

Based on a traditional folk tale from western India

A long time ago, in the ancient kingdom of Madra, which is where modern India is today, there lived a king. He and his wife had no children, although they had longed for them for many years. They decided to pray to the Sun God, Savitr, and ask him to grant them the miracle of a child.

After they had prayed to Savitr for a long time, he took pity on them and promised that a daughter would be born. In time, the baby arrived. Since she had been sent by the Sun God, he had granted her the luminous strength and grace of the sun itself. The king and queen named the new princess Savitri, after Savitr.

Young Savitri grew up to become a lovely young woman. In fact, she was so strong in character and so kind and so clever, that often the people around her felt intimidated by her gifts. It made Savitri sad that all the young men and women around her age in the kingdom were too nervous of her to even make friends.

When Savitri was old enough to travel alone, she decided to leave her kingdom. She hoped to find people who were not put off by her strength. On her travels, she passed

through a large forest. In the forest, she met a young man gathering firewood.

Savitri instantly felt that she had known this man her entire life and that they would be more than friends. She felt they would be family.

"Hello," she greeted the man. "My name is Savitri."

"I'm Satyavan," the man replied, smiling at her. "Are you new here? I haven't seen you in our woods before."

"Yes," Savitri answered. "I am on a journey around the country, but I don't have anywhere to stay this evening. Could you tell me where the nearest town is?"

"Why don't you stay with us?" Satyavan immediately suggested, for he was as taken with Savitri as she was with him. "I live with my parents in the woods. Our place isn't grand, but you are very welcome."

Savitri was thrilled that he didn't seem at all intimidated by her. "I would love to!" she replied.

Satyavan led Savitri through the woods to the humble dwelling where he lived with his parents. He introduced her to his father and mother. Savitri was astonished to learn that Satyavan's father was none other than Dyumatsena, the former king of the Salwa Kingdom, who had lost everything and gone blind.

"I believe that I am cursed," Dyumatsena told Savitri. "But if my son has the good luck to meet such a wonderful person, then I am hopeful that the curse has not passed on to him."

Savitri and Satyavan fell in love that very evening as they shared dinner with his parents. Satyavan was not intimidated by Savitri; instead, he celebrated her strength and her brains. Savitri found it easy to return the compliments, for she found him so wonderful in his own right.

Very quickly, they decided that they would like to get married. Savitri returned home to tell her parents of her decision. However, when she arrived, she found her father talking to the local wise man.

"My dear, you cannot marry Satyavan," said the king, with sad eyes. "He is indeed cursed, like his father before him. A prophecy states that he will die one year from today."

Savitri crossed her arms. "And that is supposed to mean I love him any less? I would marry him even if a prophecy said he would die tomorrow."

"You are a princess," argued the king. "You should marry someone with a great future ahead of them. Choose a different man, please."

"I love Satyavan," Savitri declared. "And whatever future we have together will be great, however short."

So, Savitri and Satyavan were married, and Savitri went to live in the woods with Satyavan and his parents. She enthusiastically joined their simple way of life, collecting fruits and spending lots of time telling stories and getting to know her new family She found that she didn't miss the trappings of her old life, because she was so happy with her husband.

She never breathed a word of the prophecy to Satyavan. So, while he happily mused about their future and what it would hold, Savitri was quietly dreading the deadline that was creeping up on them. At the end of each day, she would smile to herself as she recalled what a lovely day she had had with her husband—and then shed a single tear as she thought of the doom that had come one day closer.

Before she knew it, almost a whole year had passed, and there were only three days left before the prophecy said that Satyavan's life would be over. For those three days, Savitri fasted and did not sleep.

Her father-in-law worried about her. "You must take care of yourself," he urged her. "You mustn't give up because of Satyavan's fate."

Savitri hugged her father-in-law. "It is the opposite. I have taken an oath to fast and keep vigil, so that my soul might be as spotless as possible when Satyavan dies."

Dyumatsena didn't understand his daughter-in-law, but he left her alone after that.

On the morning when Satyavan was due to die, he went into the woods to chop firewood, as he always did. But that morning, Savitri went with him. "I feel like taking a walk," she told her unsuspecting husband.

Satyavan began to chop wood, but he soon felt unwell. "My legs are so weak, and my head aches," he groaned, stumbling.

"Lie down, my love. Take a rest until you feel better," Savitri urged him.

Satyavan did as she said, laying his head in her lap. He took one shuddering breath and then was still.

A moment later, the pitter-patter of lots of small footsteps sounded. They belonged to the servants of Yama, the god of death, who had come to collect the soul of Satyavan.

However, Savitri's goodness shone through, polished by her life of kind deeds. "You shall not take his soul," Savitri commanded, and it was as if a true goddess had spoken.

The servants retreated, confused.

A while later, Yama himself appeared. "My servants did not feel they could disobey someone so holy," he said to Savitri. "But I am the god of death, and you are a mere mortal. Satyavan's soul is mine to take."

Savitri knew that she could not fight Yama directly, so she let him pick up Satyavan. But as Yama turned to walk away, Savitri followed him.

Yama turned around. "Savitri, your husband was a good man. He will have a good life in my kingdom, I promise." He turned back around to continue on his way.

"I know he will," Savitri replied. "For you, the god of death, are wise and just."

"True," Yama called back over his shoulder. "Now, farewell. You and I are not supposed to meet for many more years."

But as Yama continued on his way, Savitri kept following.

Yama turned again, exasperated. "You cannot follow me all the way back to my realm, Savitri. Satyavan is dead."

Savitri stood her ground in front of the irritated god. "I am his wife, and my place is beside him, no matter what."

Yama turned back again, impressed by Savitri's devotion and courage. "You cannot come with him. But you are brave and strong, and so, I will grant you a wish. Anything you like, except for the life of Satyavan."

Savitri thought. "Satyavan is the only thing I want for myself. So, if you will not grant me him, I wish for my father-in-law's sight to be restored."

"You are a kind woman," said Yama. "You could have wished for riches, power, or even a new husband. Instead, you help another."

"I will do anything for those I love," Savitri replied with feeling.

Yama continued walking a short way with Savitri following, before he turned again. "To reward your good nature, I will grant you one more wish. Anything—except the life of Satyavan."

Savitri thought for a moment. "I wish for my father-in-law to have his kingdom back. It's what Satyavan would have wanted."

Yama smiled. "You really are a good person." He continued walking a short way with Savitri following. Then, he turned once more. "You are the finest mortal I have ever met. So, I will grant you one more wish. Anything—except the life of Satyavan."

Savitri considered this last wish carefully. "I can ask you for anything at all, that isn't Satyavan's life, and you have to grant it?"

"That's right," Yama confirmed.

Savitri smiled. "In that case, I wish to be the mother of Satyavan's children."

Yama frowned. "But to grant that wish, I would need to restore Satyavan to life."

"Yes, you would," Savitri replied, with another smile. "And you promised that you would grant me any wish."

Yama couldn't help but smile back at her. "Very well, Savitri, most persistent and loving of wives. I will grant you one more wish. Anything."

"Anything?" Savitri felt hope flare in her chest.

"Anything," Yama agreed.

"I wish for Satyavan to be returned to me, free of that awful curse," Savitri said, breathlessly.

"I grant you this wish," said Yama. "And I bless both of you with a long and happy life. Sit down, Savitri."

Savitri did as he said, and Yama laid Satyavan down, with his head in Savitri's lap just like before.

"I look forward to our next meeting," Yama said. "But it will not be for a very long time. Live well, determined Savitri." He walked away, disappearing among the trees.

A moment later, Satyavan woke up. "My headache is gone! How long did I sleep for?" he asked.

"Ages! You were dead to the world," Savitri told him, smiling to herself.

Together, they walked home to find that Dyumatsena could see again and had been called back to his kingdom. The whole family moved back there to live a long and happy life. The children Savitri had wished for arrived as the years passed, and Savitri took care of her whole family just as fiercely as she had fought for Satyavan's soul.

Tuya, the Clever Daughter-in-Law

Based on a story from Mongolia

A long time ago, in the land that is now Mongolia, there lived a young girl named Tuya. As soon as she was able to talk, it was clear to her parents that she was a clever girl, and by the time she had grown up, she was regularly outsmarting them.

"Tuya, you are too clever for your own good," her father would grumble.

"Yes, you should learn to take better care of the horses, instead of using your wits on us all the time," her mother would add. "You're getting a bad reputation."

Tuya just shrugged. "I can't help it!"

One day, the king rode into Tuya's village, causing a great flurry of excitement. "I've heard that there is a young girl named Tuya who lives here," he said.

Tuya's mother groaned. "Even the king has heard of your bad reputation, Tuya! I told you that nobody likes a know-it-all."

The king held up a hand. "I have heard of your wits, Tuya. Tell me, are you as clever as everybody says?"

Tuya grinned at him. "I'm even cleverer than that."

The king raised an eyebrow. "Well, let's see. I command you to find me a stick. You mustn't find it on the road, but you mustn't find it on a place that isn't a road. You can't wear your boots, but you can't go barefoot. You must come to me in neither day nor night, and when you present me with the stick, you must be neither inside nor outside. If you don't manage to complete this task, I will kill you."

Tuya's parents screamed with horror, but Tuya merely bowed to the king, looking pleased. "I will do as you command."

As dawn broke the next morning, the king was awoken by a muffled voice calling, "Your majesty! It is Tuya, and I've brought the stick you wanted."

"Where are you?" the king asked, looking around his tent.

"I am neither inside nor outside," came Tuya's triumphant reply. "I am inside the outer layer of your tent, but outside the inner layer."

"Ha!" the king clapped his hands.

"It is dawn, so neither day nor night," Tuya went on. "I am wearing my stockings, so I am neither barefoot nor in my boots."

"Ah, but where did you find the stick?" the king asked, wondering if Tuya would have fallen at the final hurdle. "Remember, it can't be a road but not not a road."

"I found it on a footpath," said Tuya.

The king laughed. "Come on in! You are the cleverest person I have ever met, and I would like to propose something to you."

Tuya skipped into the tent, looking interested.

"As you probably know, I have a son about your age, Prince Jargal," said the king. He lowered his voice. "But there is a problem. He is … not the smartest fellow, and I worry about leaving him to lead my people when I am gone. I wish to marry him to someone clever who can help guide him."

Tuya considered the king's proposal. Helping to lead the kingdom did sound more interesting than taking care of horses, even if she had to marry a stupid prince to do it. "Very well, I accept."

The king was pleased and wasted no time in introducing Tuya to Jargal. However, he knew that before they were married, he needed to see whether his son would listen to clever Tuya.

"Son, I need you to find a man of the ice and bring me his wisdom," the king said to the prince. "Only then will you have proven yourself ready to be king after me."

Jargal instantly looked troubled. His brow was furrowed as he wandered away, looking for men made of ice.

After some time, Tuya found him packing supplies and warm clothes for what looked like a long trip.

"My father needs me to find a man of the ice," Jargal told her. "I've never seen one near here, so I suppose I will have to go looking."

"You could," said Tuya, thoughtfully, "but there is a much easier way."

"What is that?" Jargal asked.

"All humans are made mostly of water, so it could be said that we are creatures of the water," Tuya explained. "And what is ice but frozen water? If we are creatures of the water, then we are also creatures of the ice. And that means that you yourself are a man of the ice."

"My goodness, you are clever!" Jargal exclaimed. He went to his father and announced, "I am a man of the ice, and the wisdom I bring you, Father, is that my bride-to-be is the cleverest person in our entire kingdom."

The king was pleased, for not only had his son listened to Tuya, but he had seen her value. The wedding took place with no further delay, and the king began to consult Tuya on all sorts of matters.

One day, the king went hunting in the lands at the edge of his kingdom. He had only planned to be gone for a couple of days, but after a week he still hadn't returned.

Jargal assumed blithely that his father had decided to hunt for a little bit longer, but Tuya was convinced something bad had happened.

On the eighth day, a group of seven riders dressed in white appeared on the horizon. As they drew close, they demanded an audience with Prince Jargal. "We have captured the king, and we are holding him for ransom!" they announced.

A wave of shock ran around the assembled people. Their king was the most fearsome monarch who had ever lived, and it was hard to imagine that he could have been taken prisoner by anyone.

"I don't believe you!" spluttered Jargal.

"He said you would say that," the lead messenger smirked. "So, he wrote this letter to prove to you that he is alive and well. Do what we say, and he will remain that way. We want you to hand over your entire kingdom to us, and then we will send your king back to you. If you refuse, he dies."

Tuya narrowed her eyes. She didn't believe them.

But Jargal was reading the letter. "This is my father's handwriting. And it sounds like he is being very well treated indeed. It sounds like such a nice place that I might even move there!"

"May I read it?" Tuya asked.

Jargal handed it over, and Tuya read:

> My dear son,
>
> As I write this, I am lying on white silk sheets, with a thick blanket of white silk on top of me. There are ten good men at my back. I have more sweet white wine than I know what to do with. In my home are seven rams. Slaughter six of them today, and then send the seventh back to where it came from. Please show this letter to your wife.
>
> Love, Father

Tuya pulled her husband to one side right away. "This letter does not mean what you think it does. Give the messengers food and wine, and call your father's advisors in for a secret meeting."

Once the prince and the advisors were assembled in a tent, Tuya waved the letter in the air. "The king is in grave danger. He is being poorly treated and sends us instructions to secure his release."

The prince and the advisors gaped at her.

"How do you know?" Jargal asked.

"Because your father has written this in a code for us to decipher," Tuya explained. "The white sheets and blanket are snow—they have left him lying in the snow. The ten good men at his back are his own fingers—they have tied his hands behind his back. The sweet white wine is his tears—he is in pain. The rams represent the messengers. He is telling us to kill six of them and use the seventh to guide us to him. We must do as he says right away and rescue him before it is too late."

Jargal and his men hurried to kill the messengers.

Once that was done, they took their clothes and six of the men dressed up as the messengers. Tuya told everyone else to dress all in white.

They made the seventh messenger lead them to where the king was being held.

As they crept close, they saw the king lying on the ground in the snow, all tied up and shivering. Tears of pain shimmered on his cheeks.

Jargal wanted to run in and free his father right away, but Tuya held him back. "Look, there are soldiers guarding him," she murmured. "We must be careful."

Indeed, there were several soldiers right next to the king and more sitting around a fire a little way away.

Tuya directed the people dressed in white to surround the area quietly, hidden against the snow. Then, the six men dressed up as the messengers walked toward where the king was being held, waving and calling greetings. Once they got close enough, they launched their attack on the unsuspecting soldiers.

The soldiers from the campfire tried to run over to help their comrades, but they were ambushed by the people in white, whom they hadn't seen against the snow.

Jargal and Tuya ran to untie the king.

"You understood!" the king cried in relief. "Well done."

"It was all Tuya," Jargal admitted, as he pulled his father to his feet and gave him a horse to ride.

"I always knew you were the cleverest person in the kingdom," cried the king. "And now you have saved it with your wits. Thank you, Tuya!"

Nayece, the Mother of All

Based on a traditional Turkana folk tale from northeastern Africa

A long time ago, in the land of Jie, which is part of the place we now know as Kenya, there lived a young girl named Nayece. Nayece's village was always busy and bustling. Her family, and all the families around, owned many cattle. Cattle were very important to the people of Jie. They were used as food and also used in place of money to buy things. So, the more cattle there were, the better for the village. Nayece, however, found it all a bit too noisy and chaotic, and she grew tired of only eating meat. She wished to live in harmony with nature in a quiet place where she could listen to the sound of the land.

So, one day, she slipped away from the busy village. Her family were alarmed when they saw that she had gone, and many search parties were sent to look for her. But Nayece was never found; it was as if she had evaporated into the air, like mist.

Many years passed, and soon the story of the missing daughter passed into legend in the village. There were few left alive who had even known Nayece. The tale was used to warn children to stay close to home and not wander into the countryside alone.

During this time, a young man was trying to build his first cattle herd. He had the most amazing silver bull, and he hoped that it would father many fine calves for him. But one morning, when he went to check the cattle, the silver bull was missing. The man searched the village and called on all his friends to ask if they had seen the silver bull. None of them had. The man's friends knew how important the bull was to him, and they vowed to help him find it.

Together, they packed food supplies of dried meats and set out to search the countryside.

"If we can't find your bull, we will find you a new one, just as good," one of the friends declared.

A little way out of the village, they found the distinctive hoofprints of the bull. "It went this way!" the young man exclaimed. "We can track him down!"

And so, they followed the tracks east across the country. They followed them into deep valleys and over high hills.

Just before sunset on the first day, they passed by another village. "Please, have you seen my silver bull?" the young man asked.

The people of the village blocked the way threateningly. "Go away. You can't have any of our bulls!" one of them said.

"I don't want your bulls!" the young man replied. "I'm searching for my bull. See these tracks I'm following? He must have passed through your village. Have any of you seen him?"

"Go away," repeated the man from the village.

The villagers rushed at the group of friends and chased them away.

The friends picked up the bull's hoofprints a little way along from the village and continued tracking, making a camp when darkness fell.

The next morning, the hoofprints were still clear as the men set off once more. The sun became hot and baking, hardening the ground and making it difficult for the men to continue on. It was much hotter than the land they were used to, and the young man worried about how his bull was faring in the heat.

As they continued on, however, it became rainy. Torrential rain fell, soaking through their clothes and making them shiver. Eventually, the hoofprints before them began to wash away. The men tried to hurry onward before they lost the trail entirely, but soon the whole thing had been wiped clean. The men were starting to feel quite hopeless. They had already run out of the food they had packed, and they couldn't see a way of getting any more.

"Look!" gasped one of the men, pointing ahead.

They were standing on one side of a tumbling hill stream that grew into a large river, which snaked through the landscape. The ground was sandy and golden, and the few green trees waved in the sweet wind, as if they were greeting the men as old friends.

The sunset bathed the whole land in a golden glow, and the group of friends thought that they had never seen anything so beautiful.

"What is this place?" the young man wondered. "It's so different from our homeland." As he pondered this question, a flash of silver on a nearby mountain slope caught his eye. He squinted, wondering if it could be what he thought it was. "Is, uh, that my bull?" he asked his friends.

"It is, I'm sure of it!" one of the others cried.

They began to hurry toward the small silver dot. Darkness fell before they managed to scale the mountain, and so the friends reluctantly made camp and vowed to begin once more at first light, hoping that the bull would also stay put during the night. Their stomachs rumbled as they settled down, and they all hoped that they would be able to turn toward home tomorrow with the silver bull in tow.

As the next day dawned, the men were up and ready in no time. To their relief, the silver bull still wandered the mountain slope above, casually grazing. As the men approached the bull, they became aware of an old woman perched on a nearby rock, watching them.

"This bull is mine," the young man said, pointing at the silver bull. "We have tracked him from the land of Jie."

The old woman shrugged. "If you say so. He has been living with me for the last couple of days."

The young man felt a little uncomfortable. He intended to take the bull home with him, but he didn't want to leave the old woman with no way of surviving. "Do you not have any cattle of your own?" he asked, looking around.

"I do not," the old woman replied.

"How do you live?" one of the friends asked, just as his stomach gave a loud rumble.

The old woman raised an eyebrow. "You are hungry? Follow me."

The group followed her over the ridge of the mountain. There, laid out before them was a lush, green valley. It looked absolutely untouched, with no signs of humans present at all. The woman led them to a bush that was heavy with golden berries hidden among papery petals. She plucked some and ate them with relish. "Try these," she encouraged the men. "They are good."

The men were unconvinced. "Berries cannot be as good as meat," the young man insisted. But when he tried the berries, he was surprised by their delicious sweetness—and by the energy he felt flooding through him.

"I used to live in Jie myself," said the old woman. "My name is Nayece. I left that land when I was quite young. I wanted to live in peace and harmony with the land. I walked until I found this valley, and I have lived here ever since. The land is so abundant that I do not need cattle to live."

The young man gasped. "I have heard stories of the lost daughter, Nayece. I can't believe it is you!"

One of the other men scoffed. "You can't expect us to believe that you have lived off these berries for your whole life."

Nayece fixed him with a sharp look. "Not just these berries, no. I have discovered many other fruits and plants that make excellent food—if you know how to cook them."

At this, some of the young men shuffled uncomfortably, for they knew nothing about cooking; but others, including the owner of the silver bull, leaned forward curiously.

Nayece smiled and said, "Follow me if you wish to learn." She led them through the valley, pointing out all of the plants that could make excellent meals. Then, she took them to the cave where she slept and showed them the easiest way to start a cooking fire.

Then, she prepared the various ingredients she had, including the berries, and she cooked the most amazing dishes for the men to try.

"Please," the young man asked. "Can you teach us what you know?"

Nayece felt glad to be asked. She felt she had uncovered the secret to living a good life from a very young age, living in harmony with the land, and she was happy to share her knowledge with these young men.

So, she spent several days teaching them all how to forage, prepare ingredients, and cook. Once the men had mastered her techniques, they decided it was time to set off for home. But as they prepared to leave, the owner of the bull hesitated.

"Mother," he said to Nayece, for this is what the group had started to call her. "This land is a paradise. It is so good, and I feel sure that our families would benefit from living the way that you do. May we bring them here to share your valley?"

Nayece thought for a moment. She had grown used to the tranquility of her valley and delighted in her quiet life. But at the same time, she knew that the young man was right—many would benefit from the fruits of the valley, and besides, she had grown to like the men and was sure their loved ones would be equally good company. "Very well," she said. "You may bring them, as long as they all abide by the ways of this valley."

So, the men left the silver bull in the valley and returned home, taking handfuls of berries with them to show the people they loved. They brought their families and their livestock to the valley, and Nayece divided the valley up into territories, so that all would have space to forage and make their homes. The people became known as the Turkana people, and Nayece was the mother of them all.